Grounding, Stranding and Wreck

by
Conrad Dixon

Ashford Press Publishing
Southampton
1988

Published by Ashford Press Publishing 1988
1 Church Road
Shedfield
Hampshire SO3 2HW

British Library Cataloguing in Publication Data

Dixon, Conrad
    Grounding, stranding and wreck.
    1. Boating — Manuals
    I. Title
    797.1

    ISBN 1-85253-075-8

Designed by Jonathan Duval
Phototypeset by Pauline Newton

Printed and bound in England by
Oxford University Press Printing House

Contents

Long-term stranding . Digging out . Shoring up .
Lifting . Lightening . Pulling and pushing .
Beaching and scuttling

List of Illustrations

Preface

THE arrival on the yachting scene of radar, satellite navigation, echo sounders and electronic logs should have greatly reduced the likelihood of boats going aground. Instead, these gadgets have induced in their owners a tendency to sail or motor at top speed in poor visibility, to navigate sloppily and to rush blindly into harbour at dusk although all the evidence is that this is when many strandings take place. Seamanship manuals have hardly anything to say about taking the ground, and there is little recognition that it is the land that often destroys ships, not the sea. One in five yacht casualties are due to a failure of anchors, chains, moorings or warps, while anchoring and mooring techniques are imperfectly understood and kedging-off is rarely practised. As a result, yachts call for help when the remedy is in the hands of the crews, and others are simply abandoned because the skipper does not know what to do.

The primary purpose of this book is to set the reader on the right train of thought when a stranding takes place, for what is done, or not done, in the first five minutes makes all the difference between minor setback and major disaster. The method used is a step-by-step approach, starting with routine grounding of craft designed for the purpose and moving on to intentional grounding for painting and maintenance. Then, by way of avoidance and miscalculation to grievous error, to serious stranding and to wreck.

The second object of this work is to give you some idea as to what steps to take down the index from a light brush with the bottom to grave danger. The message is that a proper assessment of the factors making up a contact with the sea-bed will lead to a remedy, and if the contents of this book do just that its aim will have been achieved.

CONRAD DIXON

January 1988

Grounding

The drying mooring

Thousands of boats take the ground every day. In estuaries and harbours from the Exe to Whitby, from Abersoch to Oare Creek, every soft drying patch has its quota of moorings so that bilge-keelers, centreboarders and craft fitted with legs may be seen afloat at high water and dry at low. The drying mooring has three main advantages. It is almost always cheaper than any other type; there is ready access to the bottom of the boat and its underwater fittings for painting or maintenance; and the mooring itself may be laid and tended on a do-it-yourself basis. To the advantages of cheapness and ready access may be added those of independence from busybodies and officialdom and from the kind of censorious overview sometimes exercised by boatyards or marina employees. Against this must be put the disadvantages. Your sailing is ruled by the tides, and there is constant abrasion as the boat unsticks and then returns to the bottom. Your property is more vulnerable to theft or damage, and there will be a great deal of carrying of loads across yielding ground in rubber boots and conveying mud on board. As the well-known writer Anon has it — you pays your money and you takes your choice.

In a sheltered situation with moderate rise and fall of tide the boat owner should be able to put down ground moorings virtually unaided provided, of course, that the usual permission has been obtained. For small craft the best kind is the single concrete block or clump, well dug in so that the top is flush with the surface, and provided with a cavity in the base so as to give suction and combat the pull of the riding chain. The materials for the job are set out in Fig. 1, and the method may be briefly described. Put the tobacco tin upside down in the wooden box and gradually fill the latter with concrete made from rapid-hardening cement, coarse sand and fresh water in the ratio of six of cement to eighteen of coarse sand to one of water. When mixing, make a mini-Vesuvius of sand and cement, put the water in the crater in cupfuls and shovel from the outside until the whole heap is nicely moist and even. Use the least possible amount of water to accomplish this, and when the tobacco tin has been covered put in the Lewis bolt, fill the box up to the rim and pat it down. When dry, dig it into the ground at the chosen spot. The clump or mooring block should weigh 18 kilograms for every tonne of boat it has to hold.

Fig. 1   Mooring block

materials

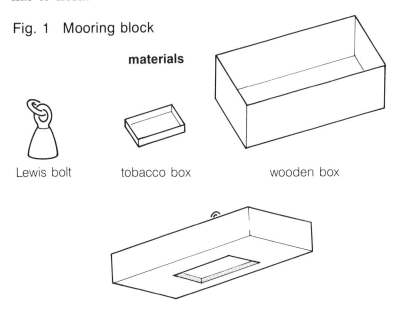

Lewis bolt   tobacco box   wooden box

With the block in position, the next step is to shackle on the mooring or riding chain. This chain should be twice as long as the depth of water at the mooring site at High Water Springs, while the riser — the rope connecting the chain to the marker buoy — must be at least the same length as the depth at High Water Springs so that the chain will always lie on the bottom when not in use. Shackles are put on with the pins done up hand-tight, well greased with Vaseline and tied in with wire or twine, as shown in Fig. 2.

Fig. 2   Moused shackle

Mousing a shackle ensures that it does not become undone by vibration or friction, while greasing the pin makes subsequent removal easier.

If the tide or current in the area is rotary in character it may be necessary to fit a swivel in the mooring to take out the kinks. Figure 3 shows what a swivel shackle looks like, and it is a matter of personal preference as to where it is positioned. You will see some swivels fitted between the clump ring and the riding chain, but I believe it best to fit them half way up the chain so that you can get to them at any time.

The concrete mooring block described here will be acceptable to authority, but some alternatives are deemed less desirable. Old gas stoves, refrigerators and tractor wheels used as sinkers for drying moorings are unsightly, inefficient and tend to damage the craft they are designed to hold.

The two-legged mooring

Where the craft to be moored is over six metres long and the selected site is known to be exposed to the vagaries of changing winds or currents it is preferable to employ the traditional two-legged mooring using anchors and chain. This system relies chiefly on

Fig. 3   Mooring swivel

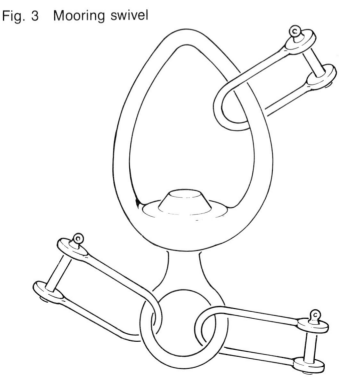

5

friction between the chain and the bottom for its holding power, and the essentials are depicted in Fig. 4. Heavy Fisherman anchors are best for the purpose, with the uppermost fluke either sawn off or hammered down. The anchors are put about 30 metres apart, and so positioned that a line joining them together will point at the prevailing wind or dominant tide. Heavy ground chains are shackled onto the anchors and joined at a ring or swivel shackle from which the riding chain will ascend.

Fig. 4   Two-legged mooring

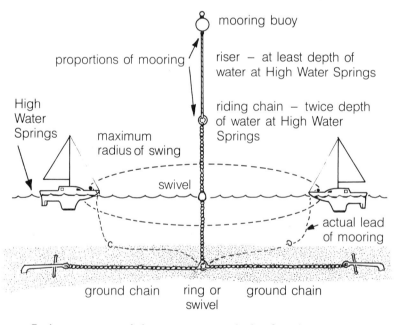

mooring buoy

proportions of mooring

riser – at least depth of water at High Water Springs

High Water Springs

maximum radius of swing

riding chain – twice depth of water at High Water Springs

swivel

actual lead of mooring

ground chain   ring or   ground chain
                    swivel

It is not essential to use new chain for the purpose; old chain from a scrapyard or marine store dealer will suffice, or you may even be lucky enough to find discarded chain in the mud from an old ships'

6

mooring. Some of this second-use chain may be what was called "black chain" because it was not galvanized but plunged red-hot into boiling tar to acquire a patina that would defeat the onset of rust or the attentions of marine creatures. Nowadays, not much "black chain" is to be seen, and the only protection available for old chain is a method developed by French fishermen. They take their ground chains home, scrub them clean in fresh water and then souse them in a container filled with used lubricating oil. It may not please the environmentalists, but it is certainly effective in keeping the chain relatively free from growths in the coming season.

The two-legged mooring can be extended to form a trot with a longer ground chain and several riding chains running off it, while in very exposed situations a second set of anchors and chains can be set at right angles to form an "X" mooring so that there is equal holding power on four quarters of the compass.

The mud berth

The "X" principle is also brought into play when a yacht is moored for the winter in a mud berth. Here the craft is put ashore in a prepared spot near the high water mark where the owner has previously dug a hole in the saltings to accommodate the keel and/or skeg. (See Fig. 5.) When in position, the hull is tied to four stakes so placed as to hold it in the berth. The hard part is getting the keel into its trench, and the best method is to outline the patch of ground where the yacht will lie with canes or withies so that when the times comes the boat can be fitted into a kind of framework shadowing the shape of the hull. It also

Fig. 5   The mud berth

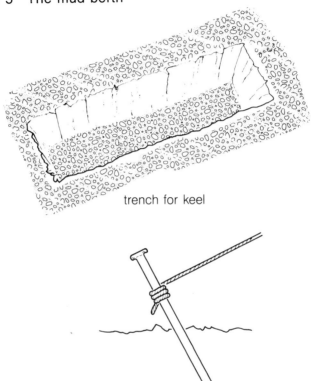

trench for keel

mooring stake

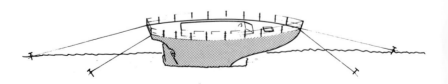

helps to have hammered in the stakes beforehand and to get some friends in hip boots standing by to take lines. Once in the mud berth, the hull is only at risk of breaking free for a few hours a month, for most of the time the water will not come high enough to do any harm.

Grounding by design

This usually takes one of two forms. As the purpose is to make repairs, do some maintenance or paint ship, it is a question of either selecting a good spot on a shingle bank or sandy beach or positioning the yacht alongside a wall, wharf or post. The problem in the first case is to avoid damage by abrasion as it settles and comes off, and in the second instance to prevent the boat falling over at low water so that a lot of impact damage ensues.

On the beach

Certain sheltered beaches and banks of sand and shingle are recognized spots for putting on antifouling or doing underwater repairs, and it will do no harm to enquire in the first instance of the wise old men who prop up the bar in yachting clubs or pubs about any soft spots, protruding obstacles or tidal anomalies that may exist in the chosen place. Next, you must establish for yourself the precise time of high water and confirm that this is a period of ''making'' tides with a higher level on Thursday than that of Wednesday. If you don't take this elementary precaution there is the possibility of being ''neaped'' and not getting afloat again for up to a fortnight.

Fig. 6 Going on

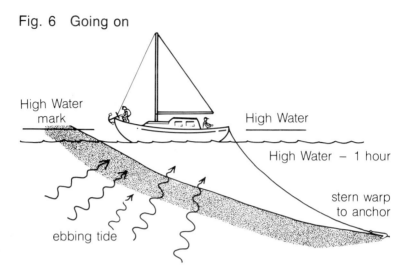

The surest way of being certain of a "making" tide is to look at the very useful quick-reference card supplied with *Reed's Nautical Almanac*, which has a red line under the daily entries for Dover. A longer line on Thursday than on Wednesday is what you're looking for.

It is also important to make a mental estimate as to how long you need to be aground, and to time events accordingly. For example, if it is merely a matter of cutting a line from a propeller shaft or unblocking a water intake it may only be necessary to be aground for two or three hours each side of low water, while for antifouling you'll probably want all the time you can get. In this latter case, the time to go on is about an hour after high water — as in Fig. 6. Motor or sail in very slowly, stemming the tide, and drop a stern anchor so as to have extra control when the moment of grounding takes place. The anchor will prevent pivoting and give the chance of hauling off for a second try if the first spot proves ill chosen. When the stem or keel has "bitten" and taken hold, the forward crewman in Fig. 6 should splash ashore with the main anchor to prevent the craft ranging about and abrading the keel. Shift weights or put the boom over so that the boat lies on the side *not* to be worked on — as in Fig. 7.

Fig. 7   Painting between tides

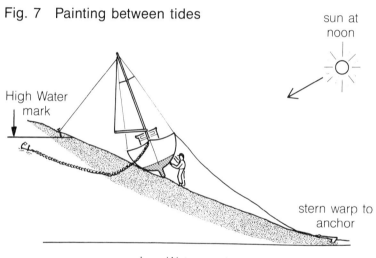

sun at noon

High Water mark

stern warp to anchor

Low Water mark

   In this illustration a round-bilge motor-sailer is being painted between tides, and the extra precaution has been taken of running the main halliard off to a stake so as to make absolutely sure that the craft settles the right way. Naturally, this sort of work is best done on days with morning and evening high tides, and in Fig. 7 the owner has also made sure that the midday sun is at right-angles to the side being painted so that it has every chance to dry before the water returns.

Drying out on a wall or wharf

Where the underwater profile of a yacht does not lend itself to drying out on a beach the alternative is to prop it up against a wall or wharf. In Fig. 8 a racing craft with a "champagne glass" configuration is shown on one side and a fin and skeg cruiser on the other. Both boats are listed inwards by between 5° and 10° — an amount that ensures that they will not fall away from the wall but are not at such an extreme angle as to damage the standing rigging. The bases of this kind of drying berth are not necessarily coincident with the low water mark, and it will often be essential to use the Twelfths Rule to ascertain when the boat is going to touch and the crew will need to distribute weight and put out securing lines.

Fig. 8   Drying out on a wall or wharf

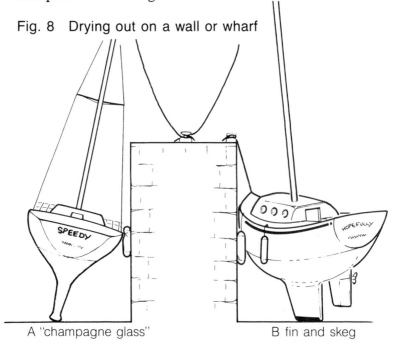

A "champagne glass"   B fin and skeg

The Twelfths Rule

The Twelfths Rule is based on the premise that in the six hours between high water and low water at any particular place the depth changes follow this ratio:

	Fall
High water to high water + 1 hour	1/12th of depth
High water + 1 hour to high water + 2 hours	2/12ths of depth
High water + 2 hours to high water + 3 hours	3/12ths of depth
High water + 3 hours to high water + 4 hours	3/12ths of depth
High water + 4 hours to high water + 5 hours	2/12ths of depth
High water + 5 hours to high water + 6 hours	1/12th of depth

Thus, if the range of tide on a certain day is 6 metres, the rate of fall of the tide will be:

HW to HW + 1	=	0.5	metres
HW + 1 to HW + 2	=	1	metre
HW + 2 to HW + 3	=	1.5	metres
HW + 3 to HW + 4	=	1.5	metres
HW + 4 to HW + 5	=	1	metre
HW + 5 to HW + 6	=	0.5	metres
Total		6	metres

A boat drawing 1.5 metres will, therefore, take the ground at about two hours before low water *if* the ground at the foot of the wall is the same as the low water mark. However, if, as is so often the case, the ground at the base of the wharf is above the low water mark the boat will ground sooner. Let us say that the foot of the wharf dries 1.5 metres. Add this to the draft of the yacht to make 3 metres, and it will be seen that the boat will dry out at half ebb, three hours after high water, and be aground for six hours. Of

13

course, only four of those hours will be available for work — the last two of the ebb tide and the first two of the flood.

Fig. 9   Lead and line and sounding pole

lead and line for sounding round the yacht

one knot for draught of yacht

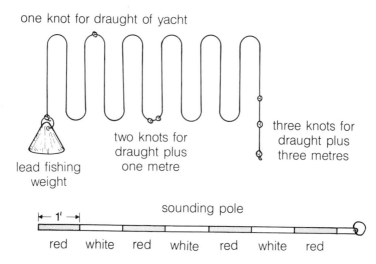

lead fishing
weight

two knots for
draught plus
one metre

three knots for
draught plus
three metres

sounding pole

|← 1' →|

red   white   red   white   red   white   red

Checking the depth

It will be appreciated that as tide tables are founded on guesstimates compiled from past observations, and the Twelfths Rule is an inexact average, more precise means will be needed to get the timing right for a keel yacht to touch bottom. The deep-sea lead of the past is insufficiently closely defined for the job, but owners may make their own small sounding kits for this purpose, and for finding depth in less-controlled circumstances. The top part of Fig. 9 shows a lead and line made from a fishing weight and some knotted codline, with marks for draught, draught plus one metre and draught plus three metres. The sounding pole of red-and-white-painted bamboo is marked in feet, and stows out on an outer shroud when not in use. By using these simple devices it will be relatively easy to know within an inch or two when the lowest part of the keel is about to touch bottom.

The grounding angle

To achieve an inclined angle of between 5° and 10° it is often helpful to send a crewman along the quay to signal when there is a sufficient inward lean of the mast. Standing on the side of the boat nearest the supporting wall or wharf may be enough to get the right inclination; the boom may be swung over to help, and in those obstinately stiff craft that are slow to lean it may be necessary to fasten a water container to the outboard end of the boom or carry a halliard ashore to a bollard and suspend a weight from it. The only other problem likely to arise at this stage is that some yachts have cut-away keels so that they lean forward alarmingly when they dry out. This can be cured by holding the bows up with mooring warps — as shown in Fig. 8.

Fendering

The pressure exerted by a leaning boat is considerable, and adequate — not to say heavy — fendering is a must. Figure 10 embodies some suggestions. Motor-car tyre fenders squash well and protect topsides; they have to be covered with sacking to keep black marks at bay, and the drainage hole in the lowest part stops them accumulating pints of dirty water which spurt

Fig. 10 Types of fender

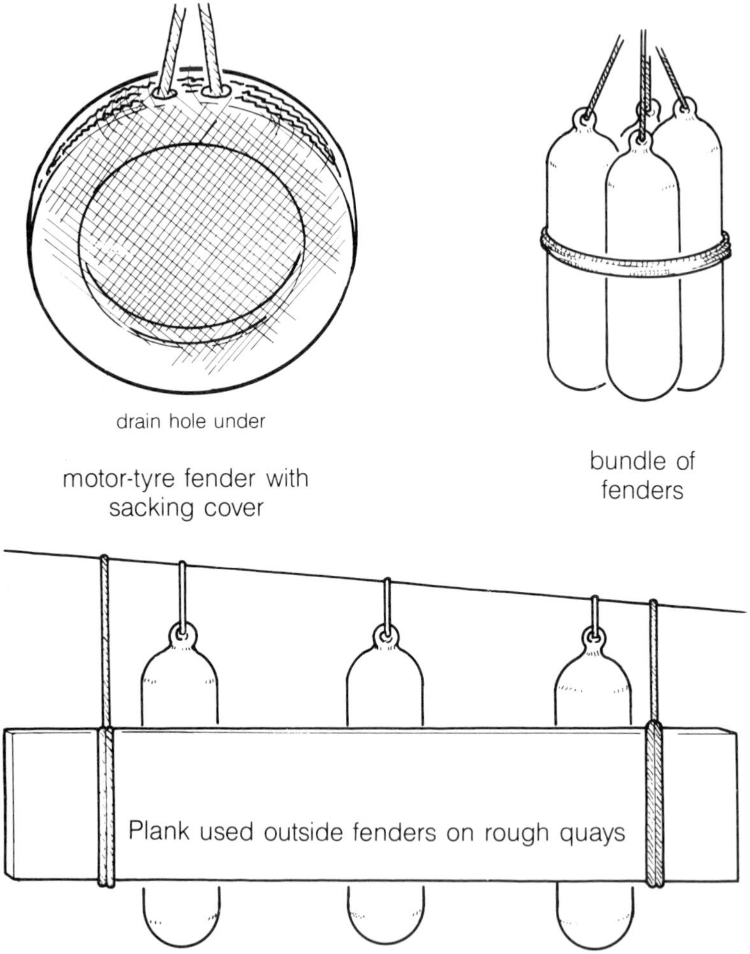

drain hole under

motor-tyre fender with
sacking cover

bundle of
fenders

Plank used outside fenders on rough quays

out when they are brought on deck. A bundle of
fenders will stand being squeezed when a single one
will pop; and if the quay or wall surface is rough a
plank on the outside protects the fenders from deep
scratches and embedded dirt which later transfers to
the topsides.

Bilge-keelers and centreboarders

Craft fitted with bilge keels may be maintained or painted on any firm drying surface, for the only difficulty that is likely to arise is when one keel finds a soft patch so that an awkward angle develops. The centreboarder can be more of a problem. As may be seen in Fig. 11, this type hugs the ground and it is hard to get to the garboard strake — the part of the hull nearest the keel. Small centreboarders may be levered to lie on one side and then the other, but substantial hulls will have to be painted on a grid where the wielders of brushes may get between the supporting timbers and reach all parts of the bottom.

Legs

Some keeled craft — mostly those with wooden hulls — are fitted permanently with legs. These may take the form of baulks of timber with their upper ends bolted onto or through the hull, or be made of tubular steel. The legs are guyed fore and aft to keep them rigid, and terminate in flat plates that stop them

Fig. 11   Centreboarder and bilge-keeler

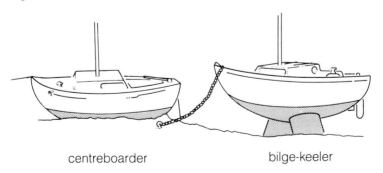

centreboarder   bilge-keeler

sinking into the mud. The tubular steel type of legs
are adjustable to cope with hard and soft ground,
while both types either unbolt altogether or are hinged
to fold back along the hull in the same way as
leeboards fitted to barges. The most important thing to

Fig. 12   Legs

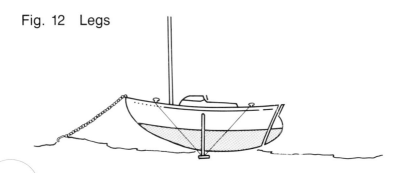

remember when dealing with legs is to get the angle
right. In Fig. 13 the correct method is shown on the
right-hand side of the drawing where the legs are
made to splay outwards so that stability is achieved.

Fig. 13   Right and wrong angles for legs

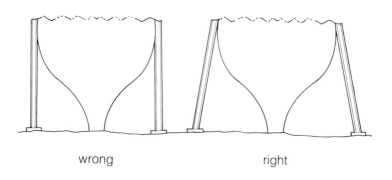

wrong   right

Grounding alongside other vessels

It is often tempting when berthing in a strange harbour to go alongside another vessel. In a tidal port there seems to be an advantage in that the other man will tend the lines as both craft sink down onto the bottom, but there are two dangers to bear in mind. The craft may be a long-term resident, such as a dredger, out-of-season excursion boat, spare harbour tug or fishing trawler under repair, and it will have formed a ''gutter'' with its keel. Consequently, it will stay upright at low water while you will go down to a much lower position.

Fig. 14   Caught under the bilge

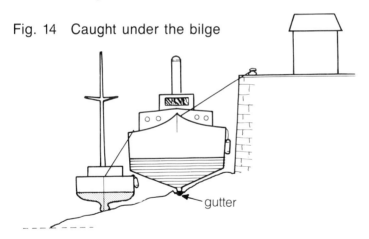

gutter

The danger outlined in Fig. 14 arises when the flood tide begins to make. The yacht has become trapped under the bilge of its larger neighbour, and damage to rails, rigging and topsides may result. Conversely, in Fig. 15 a visiting yacht has berthed alongside a flat-bottomed craft and has made the assumption that because it *is* flat-bottomed it will itself settle down on a level plane. At low water the barge

19

has adapted to the incline of the drying ground and has actually pushed the yacht into both a dangerous and potentially damaging situation. The message from both examples is clear. Do not moor alongside craft in drying harbours unless (a) you are of roughly the same size and underwater profile, (b) the ground is flat, or nearly so, and (c) the bottom is soft enough to keep you upright when the water has drained away.

Fig. 15   Pushed over by a barge

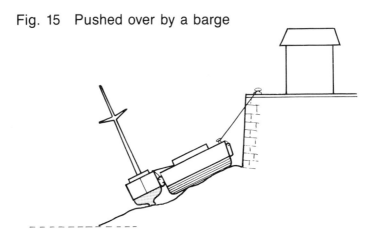

Anchors and cables

Cruising boats use their anchors constantly as *the* means of avoiding taking the ground, and what follows is an assessment of the equipment available, an account of the techniques to employ and the remedies to use when things go wrong. Ever since St Paul was wrecked on his way to Rome the correct use of anchors has been an essential part of good seamanship, and although in his case the equipment was most likely stones with holes in them secured by plaited ropes, the apprehensions and actions of those aboard were just the same then as now. The crew of St Paul's ship:

> 'sounded and found it twenty fathoms; and when they had gone a little further, they sounded again, and found it fifteen fathoms. Then fearing lest we should have fallen upon rocks, they cast four anchors out of the stern, and wished for the day.'

Anchor types

Six varieties of anchor in current use appear in Fig. 16. The choice of an anchor or anchors rests chiefly on striking a balance between holding power, weight and ease of stowage, for the various types have different properties so that, to a large extent, where you will be using your anchor dictates the selection. The Fisherman, the oldest of the six, holds well in everything except soft mud and hard rock, but it tends to capsize because its arms are relatively short and so catch the chain round the upturned fluke at the turn of the tide. It is also awkward to stow, although yachts with a stemhead roller are able to position it with the shank on the roller, the flukes outboard and vertical, and the stock flat on the deck.

The CQR and the Bruce hold well in soft mud or sand, but stow with difficulty, while the Sea Grip works well on rock and weed, but must generally be folded for stowage. The Stockless and Danforth fit into a hawsepipe, but the former tends to pick up balls of mud or clay and skate along the bottom without taking hold.

Fig. 16 Anchors

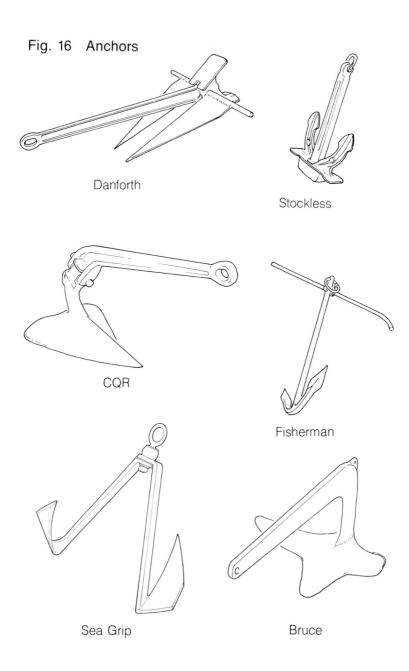

Danforth

Stockless

CQR

Fisherman

Sea Grip

Bruce

My personal preference is for the Danforth because it has the best ratio of holding power to weight — about 14:1 — and is stockless for easy housing. The tumbling flukes ensure that it works whichever way it lands on the bottom, while the long bar running through the flukes acts as a stock but does not get in the way as, for example, the Fisherman anchor stock tends to do.

How many anchors should a cruising yacht carry, and what type should they be? My choice is a Danforth as main bower, a CQR as the kedge and a Sea Grip as spare.

Weights of anchor and chain

The weight of anchor and size of chain should be proportionate to the size of the boat, and while it is wise not to be dogmatic about the choice of ground tackle, it would be foolish not to lay down a safe weight and size standard. The following table may be of help.

Yacht length (metres)	Anchor weight (kilograms)	Chain size (millimetres)	Chain size (inches)
5	7	8	5/16ths
7	10	8	5/16ths
9	12	9	3/8ths
12	16	9	3/8ths
15	23	10	7/16ths

Strength of chain

This is obtained from the formula:

$$\frac{(\text{Diameter in 1/8ths of an inch})^2}{10} = \text{working strain in tons;}$$

so that for 3/8th inch chain used on a boat 9 metres in length we get:

$$\frac{3^2}{10} \text{ working strain, which equals 9/10ths of a ton.}$$

The breaking strain is working strain × 4, which gives:

$$\frac{36}{10} \text{ or about 3½ tons as the breaking strain.}$$

Naturally, when chain is under pressure it parts at the weakest point and, with one exception shortly to be dealt with, the weak point tends to be the joining shackle.

Breaking strain and pile moorings

There is only one occasion when breaking strain is of real importance, and that is where pile moorings are concerned. Piles are rigid with no "give" in them, and a chain is put under greatest strain when subjected to a sharp plucking movement caused by wind and wave. In Fig. 17 the bow of a yacht is shown secured by chain through the stemhead to a sliding ring fitted to a bar attached to a pile driven into the sea bed. The up-and-down movement at the bow puts severe wrenching strains on the links, and in the lower half of the drawing elasticity has been restored by using some chain and the rest 20 mm multiplait with a great deal of "give" in it.

Single fastenings are always suspect with pile moorings, and in Fig. 18 a yacht is shown secured with double warps and chains fore and aft. Never be tempted to use rope alone when making fast to piles; the chafe factor is such that the warps will rub through in short order. The chain used on pile moorings for attachment to the sliding ring should have the same breaking strain as for your main anchor. Fit a lesser size and you will be asking for trouble.

Fig. 17   Securing to pile moorings

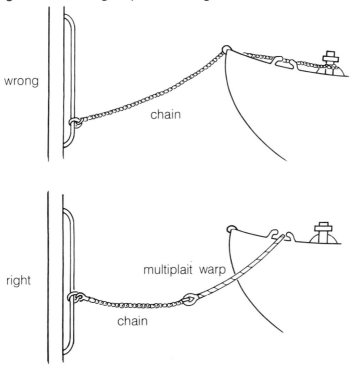

25

Fig. 18   Mooring on piles

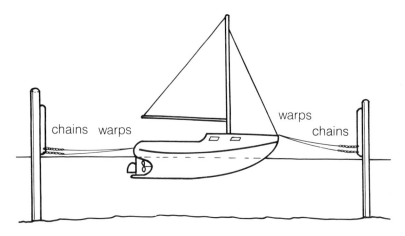

Length of chain

Anchor chain is usually sold in lengths of 15 fathoms or 27½ metres, and for yachts accustomed to mooring. in shallow water a 15-fathom length will suffice for the main anchor. The classic ratio between depth and length of chain is that the amount of chain let out should be at least three times the greatest anticipated depth. Thus, at a sheltered anchorage where the depth at low water will be a fathom and at high water three fathoms, the master of the yacht should order that at least nine fathoms of chain be let out when anchoring. Of course, this ratio is a bare minimum for use in the lightest of weather and, if there is enough swinging room, twelve fathoms would be better. Yachts that cruise around the Channel Islands, the West Country or the Brittany coast, where the tidal range is considerable and the anchorages are deep, would need to carry two joined lengths of chain for the main anchor, giving a scope of 30 fathoms or 55 metres. The kedge anchor requires at least five metres of chain, and preferably ten, before a length of warp is shackled on, as does the spare. The chain serves the dual purpose of helping to keep the stock horizontal and avoiding severance of the warp on a jagged bottom.

Fig. 19   Yawing at a single anchor

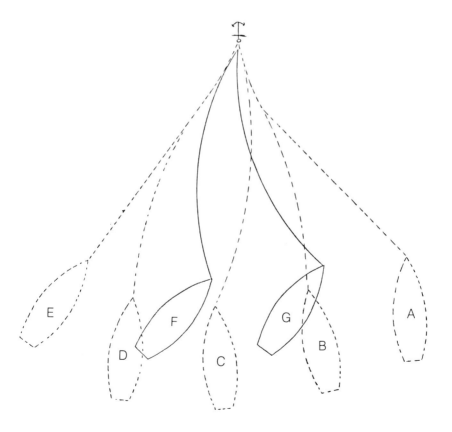

Holding power of an anchor

The theoretical holding power of an anchor can be expressed in relation to its weight with, for example, the anchor of an eighteenth-century man-of-war registering 3:1 and a modern Danforth 14:1; but from the practical point of view, what makes an anchor hold is the angle of the shank to the chain and its resistance to the sideways wrenching force called yawing. Ideally, the angle between the shank of an anchor and its chain should be 180° so that there is no upward lift to reduce holding power, for once the shank begins to lift even a few degrees from the horizontal much of its power is lost. In short, the longer the chain on the bottom the better the holding power of an anchor.

Yawing is a phenomenon induced by wind and wave, and its effect may be seen in Fig. 19. The boat swings from right to left (from A to E) under the influence of the elements, and then surges up to windward at points F and G before falling back on the restraining chain. It is at this fall-back stage that anchors will loosen their hold and tend to drag.

The dragging anchor

In the open sea or the mouth of a large estuary no corrective action need be taken provided that there is clear ground and clear water down-wind or down-tide, and that the depth does not greatly alter. The two signs of a dragging anchor are the grating noise felt, or sometimes heard, as you put a hand or ear to the cable, and a significant change in the anchor bearing.

It is good seamanship to take the angle of shore

objects when anchoring, and in Fig. 20 a yacht that has anchored with a pier to starboard and a dolphin to port notes that the relative angle between the fore-and-aft line and these objects has decreased significantly with a rising wind. The same change would be noted if the bearings were taken by hand-bearing compass and logged in degrees. With little room down-wind, it is necessary to first pay out more chain and then consider letting down either a weight on that chain to keep it closer to the sea bed, or a second anchor. If yawing is a problem, this second anchor should be put down at the extremity of the yaw so as to be clear of the first. Few yachts nowadays carry a weight and collar for slipping down the main chain to get extra friction by keeping more of it on the bottom, but a spare anchor on an oversized shackle fitted around the cable may be lowered on a warp to the bottom to do the job. In effect, this will achieve tandem anchors — a means of getting better holding power that will be referred to later on.

The dragging chain

The anchor cable, minus the anchor itself, can be used to heave-to in open water with a good fetch down-wind. Paying out all the main cable so that it drags along the bottom will keep a boat's head to wind most effectively while the crew cooks a meal or makes repairs. Recovery is easy, and the rate of down-wind drift will be no more than a knot or two in anything short of a full gale.

Fig. 20   Anchor bearings

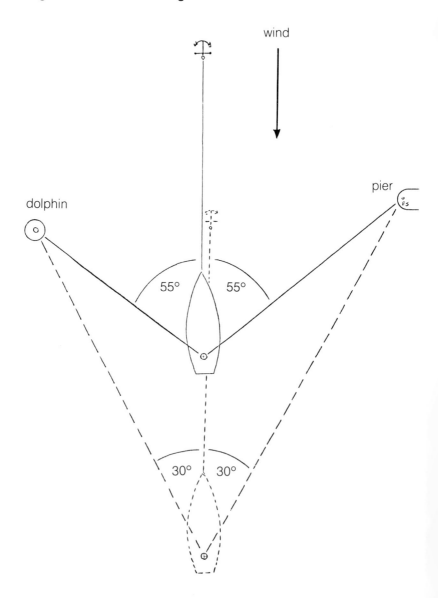

Anchoring to take the ground

Where the intention is to anchor the craft in order
that it will take the ground, the two things to look out
for are that the selected position be attained, and
swing and abrasion reduced to a minimum. In Fig. 21
the skipper of a bilge-keeler, who at dusk and half-
ebb wanted to lie aground for most of the night
between two sheltering sandbanks, finds that, at
midnight, a wind change has put his craft askew on
one of them. To be certain of achieving the right
position he should have employed a running moor to
restrict the radius of movement as the tide went
down.

The running moor

The running moor, which is also called the flying
moor, is a means of securing a boat between two
anchors so as to give a small swinging circle, and it is
particularly useful in confined spaces where a tide or
current flows first one way and then the other. The
bow anchor is known as the riding anchor and the
stern as the lee or sleeping anchor, and the key to
success lies in getting the stern or kedge anchor ready
beforehand with the cable leading through a fairlead
and the bitter, or inboard, end made fast.

Drop the kedge and motor or sail slowly until the
whole of its cable has been paid out and the boat pulls
up with a jerk. (See the top part of Fig. 22.) The
kedge being firmly embedded, you may now put
down the bow or riding anchor and haul back on the
kedge or lee warp so that you are, as the saying goes,
"middle for diddle" and half way between the two

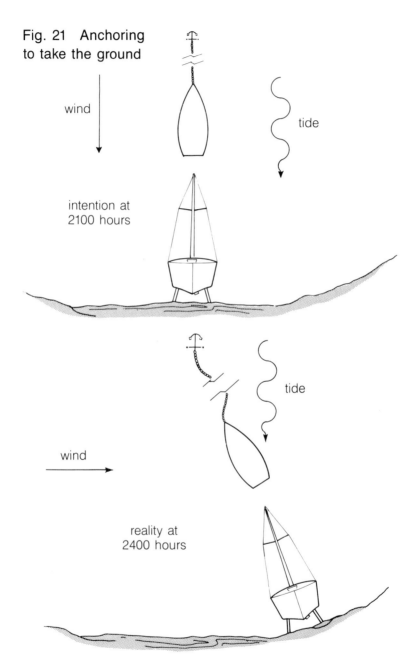

Fig. 21 Anchoring
to take the ground

wind

tide

intention at
2100 hours

tide

wind

reality at
2400 hours

Fig. 22 The running moor

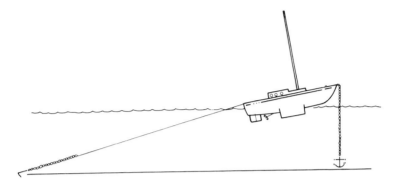

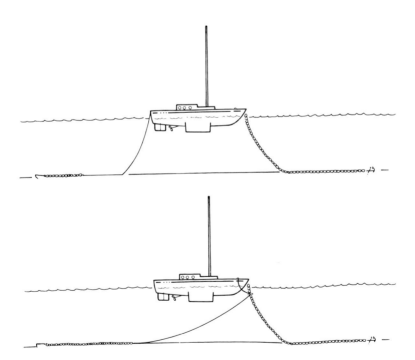

Fig. 23 Running moor, third anchor and anchors in tandem

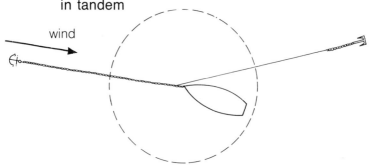

wind

running moor: radius of swinging room

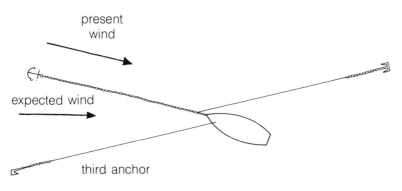

present
wind

expected wind

third anchor

deployment of the third anchor

anchors in tandem

anchors with an equal amount of cable out on both. When the boat has settled down, take the cable of the lee anchor forward, tie it with a rolling hitch to the main chain and bring the end of the warp inboard, as in the third part of Fig. 22.

When unmooring, the direction of wind or tide will dictate which anchor comes up first. With the wind or tide ahead fall back on the main or bow cable until the kedge can be plucked vertically from the ground; if wind and tide are astern try it t'other way. Of course, you will need to separate the lee anchor cable from its opposite number before attempting to recover either anchor. The principal advantage of the running moor is shown in the top drawing of Fig. 23. Compared to the position at single anchor, the swinging radius is much reduced.

Deployment of the third anchor

Let us assume that your craft has taken up the position set out in the top drawing in Fig. 23, and that a gentle west-north-west wind is keeping the boat within the small swinging circle. A weather forecast is received to the effect that the wind is going to back westerly and increasing in strength. The correct response is to put out the third anchor by dinghy in the place where it will do most good, and the final deployment is shown in the second part of Fig. 23. The angle made with the lie of the main cable is about 30°, and the expected wind bisects that angle. Yawing may be greatly reduced by taking the cable of the kedge or lee anchor back to the stern of the boat.

Anchors in tandem

When a severe blow is forecast from a particular quarter it may be prudent to re-lay the main anchor with a back-up, and the arrangement is set out in the third part of Fig. 23. The CQR normally used as a kedge is detached from its warp, so that the five or ten metres of ground chain may be shackled onto the ring of the main anchor — in this case a Fisherman. The advantage is that the main anchor has restraint ahead and astern of it so that the hold is less likely to be dislodged by direct pull or yawing.

Anchor buoys and tripping lines

So far, we have not looked at the type of ground which is festooned with old chains, rusty wires or discarded nets, but it is a fact of life that popular anchoring spots are often littered with such debris and that anchors become fouled, making recovery difficult. The orthodox answer is to use anchor buoys with tripping lines, and Fig. 24 shows tripping lines made fast to the crowns of both anchors.

Fig. 24   Anchor buoys and tripping lines

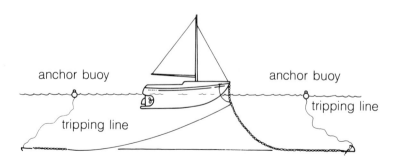

Unfortunately, the cure is sometimes worse than the disease, for tripping lines often foul stern gear at low water and the change of tide so that a wrap-round of propeller or rudder takes place with consequent labour to clear them. The best place for a tripping line is not on a buoy at all but made fast to the cable below the water line — as in Fig. 25. The way to get the

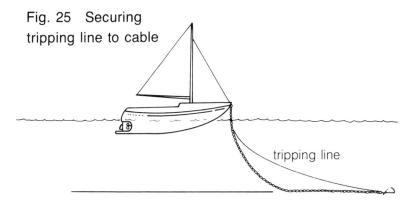

Fig. 25 Securing tripping line to cable

tripping line

tripping line in this position is to have one crewman lowering the anchor and another tending the line so that they do not get tangled. When the anchor cable is nearly all the way out, tie the tripping line to it and lower away another couple of metres of chain or warp.

The tripping line needs several desirable properties. It must be strong enough to lift the anchor vertically; long enough to reach the surface at any state of tide; and must not float. Attaching the line to the anchor so that *it* does not foul anything may require some thought. With the CQR it is made fast to the ring on top of the fixed arm, while with a Fisherman it clove-hitches round the crown with one or two back-hitches to finish off. The Bruce has a hole at the end of the stock, and the tripping line is probably best shackled on at this point. The Sea Grip cannot take a tripping line, while Stockless and Danforth anchors have tumbling flukes that have a tendency to jam on lines tied to the crown. The careful owner puts a stiff wire strop on the crown and ties the tripping line to it.

Clearing a fouled anchor

Most sailors will be familiar with the notion that the bitter end of an anchor cable — the inboard end most distant from the anchor — should be attached to a strongpoint in the locker by cord or codline so that, in emergency, it can be cut and the cable allowed to run out. A logical extension of the idea is that the securing line be long enough so that the bitter end may be brought out on deck *before* the line is slashed through, ·

Fig. 26   Butcher's hook used to clear fouled anchor

for that way you can either buoy the chain for subsequent recovery or take it elsewhere — often by dinghy — to get a pull in another direction.

Anchors tend either to get wedged or to lodge underneath something on the sea-bed, and in the former case the best technique is to motor round in circles and pull it out by brute force. The lodged anchor requires hauling up tight on the chain at low water with everybody on the foredeck to depress the bows, and then trying a range of solutions starting with quick lowering and raising and a transfer of weight fore and aft in the hope of dislodging the flukes. The next move is to get hold of the obstruction and haul up tight while the anchor is lowered down and away from it. A boathook may sometimes work, or passing a rope under the obstacle, but my favourite is the S-shaped hook normally used to hold carcasses on overhead rails in butchers' shops. The hook is attached to a line, and the obstacle is "fished" for until the hook engages. When the line is as tight as may be, the anchor can be lowered and manoeuvred free. Fig. 26 demonstrates what is to be done, and the great advantage is that if, as so often happens, the grappling device has to be abandoned because *it* in turn has become tangled with the wreckage, the line can be cut and the hook sacrificed.

Many methods using grapnels, spring-loaded buoy catchers or fenders for holding up foul chain result in the recovery of the anchor, but also the loss of much of the gear used, and that gear then contributes further to the foulness of the anchorage.

The next step

Voluntary grounding, and the means of preventing stranding, have been explored, and the controlled phase may be said to be over. So far, the skipper and his crew have been chiefly in command of the situation and able to plan ahead: hereafter their instinctive reaction to external forces will slowly begin to dominate the narrative.

Stranding

The four factors

In the early stages of a stranding the skipper will want to know four things. The sea state and the wind direction will have been at the forefront of his mind since the voyage commenced, but the additional information he now requires is the underwater shape of his boat and the nature of the bottom on which it has stranded.

Knowledge of underwater profile

The underwater silhouette of a boat will often dictate the line of action to be followed when it strands, and there are seven main types of hull. They are:

1 The long, straight keel. Typically, the converted lifeboat, fishing vessel and many motor-sailers.

2 The bilge-keeler — either with a central keel and two fins, or having two bilge-keels and no central keel.

3 A short-keel sailing boat, usually with the greatest depth at the after end of the keel.

4 A sloping keel — invariably with the greatest depth towards the stern of the boat.

5 Fin and skeg, with the fin generally deeper.

6 Catamarans. Both keels of equal depth.

7 Trimarans, with the central hull generally having the greatest depth.

It is only prudent to have the underwater profile of your craft recorded in the log, either as a drawing or in the form of a photograph taken when hauled out. Naturally, the sketch or photo should be so placed in the log book that the water line is precisely horizontal.

Knowledge of the bottom

This may sometimes be ascertained just by looking at the chart, but an alternative is to dab at the bottom with a grease-smeared sounding pole or a lead "armed" with grease in the hollow at the base. The significance of knowing the nature of the ground cannot be over-estimated, and some examples follow of how knowledge of the bottom dictates subsequent action.

Let me start with the most obvious case. The boat has slowly ground to a halt in deep mud, with only the deadness of the water alongside and the lack of movement to signal a stranding. Three pieces of information are immediately available. The keel, or keels, are likely to have dug a "gutter" so that they could be anything up to six inches into the surface. The easiest way off is certain to be back the same way she went on, and any pulling or pushing effort should be channelled in that direction. The rudder had best be kept on the same heading as it was when the stranding took place. Shingle or gravel indicates that anchors may only hold with difficulty, while rock means that abrasion is the chief danger if any sort of sea is running. Boulders will endanger parts of the hull *above* the keel, while sharp, broken shell will cut unprotected feet. Weed endangers propellers and rudders, while ooze may engulf crewmen who leap overboard to lighten ship or try to push her off. Knowledge that the ground is firm, level sand is useful to the centreboarder that touches lightly upon it, for a quick haul-up of the plate and a U-turn gets it out of danger. The gradient and extent of a shoal are worth knowing, for the vessel that touches near the peak will keep sail set and try to bump over, while another that is nudging the foothills will give up and go another way. Let us start with the easiest case of all — the yacht that strands gently on a soft spot during a rising tide, and which is in minimum peril.

Calm water solution (rising tide)

This yacht was moving slowly up a sheltered river at half-flood and with the wind off the land when she stranded. There is deeper water down-wind and, although an initial burst of engine astern has failed to move her, the ground is soft mud and the boat is on the tip of a shoal. Figure 27 embodies the range of

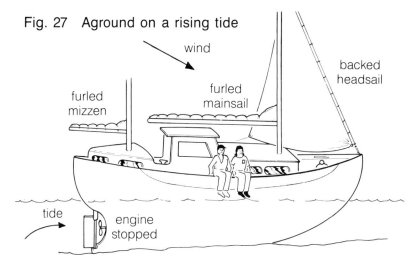

Fig. 27   Aground on a rising tide

wind

backed
headsail

furled
mainsail

furled
mizzen

tide

engine
stopped

action required. The engine has now been stopped to prevent the passage of material in suspension through the cooling system, and the rudder has been put to starboard in order that the flowing tide will push the head that way if the ketch comes unstuck all of a sudden. Ensuing action may be summarized under do's and don'ts.

Do	*Don't*
Go about on the other tack if the wind will thereby tend to push you into deeper water. In very calm conditions, harden mainsail and mizzen, and rock boat from side to side to break suction (this is called "sugging").	Drop an anchor under the forefoot, as you may well run over it when the boat moves and do some damage. Also, it may be awkward to recover — especially if the cable gets trapped under the keel when movement occurs.
Pole off, using long boathook or a spinnaker pole.	Head the craft farther inshore so that it may touch again after becoming free.
Back the headsail, as in Fig. 27, so that the wind will drive the head towards deeper water.	Start the engine until the hull is free and the propeller can rotate without stirring up silt that will be taken in by the cooling system.
Lower main and mizzen and swing the booms outboard to cant or heel the ship over and reduce draught.	Try heeling with a bilge-keeler because that will *increase* the draught.

Put crewmen on the side rails for the same purpose.

Reply courteously to VHF calls from passing craft offering assistance, and say that your boat is in no danger at present. Make the same response to a runabout that has pulled alongside to offer (a) a tow, and (b) to run off a kedge anchor.

Forget that you may *have* to put out a kedge, as described later, if the wind changes and persists in pushing the boat farther inshore.

Calm water solution (falling tide)

Speed is of the essence, and the appreciation of the situation must be rapid indeed. More sail, or more engine, and heeling may do the trick, and a shift of weight is often essential. In Fig. 28 two craft have

Fig. 28 Weight forward and full astern

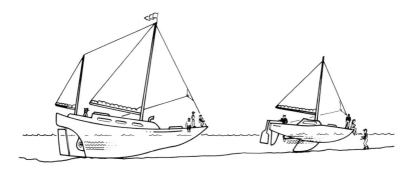

45

stranded on a gently shelving shore with the tide on the way out. Both are going full astern and have transferred crew to the bow to lessen pressure of the keel on the bottom. The lighter craft on the right has also put a man into the water to lighten ship and shove her astern. It must be appreciated that the amount of power available from an engine driving a propeller in reverse is only between 60% and 80% of the power available when the screw is running in the normal mode. The do's and don'ts are:

Do	*Don't*
Give the engine a thrashing — full power while the odds on coming off are best.	Ignore the temperature gauge, for overheating may take place if the intakes get clogged.
Stow sail, unless it is a helpful wind.	Let sheets trail in the water. At this stage the last thing required is a rope round the screw.
Try both side-to-side rocking and a transfer of weight from forward to aft.	Leave it too long before thinking about kedging-off. In general, it is unwise to waste more than five minutes on the preliminary do's: then go all out for kedging-off.
Utilize any wave action by timing bursts of power with an incoming roller.	
Get as many of the crew off the boat as possible. Those that are not acting as mobile ballast up at the bow should be either in a dinghy or over the	Send a distress call for, after all, you are *not* in grave and imminent danger and do not require

side. Both categories will need to have well-shod feet and wear buoyancy aids.

Accept, with thanks, any offers from amateur sailors passing by to lay out a kedge or attempt to tow you off. Naturally, use own kedge, cable and warp for the purpose.

assistance urgently. A VHF call to a friend or boatyard to get a pluck off is perfectly permissible.

Tideless water solution

With no help, and no hindrance, from the tide there are two techniques worth bearing in mind. Heeling or canting the hull to reduce draught may be accomplished by putting out an anchor at right-angles to the fore-and-aft line and then making a halliard fast to the cable — as in Fig. 29. By winding in the

Fig. 29   Heeling the hull with a beam anchor

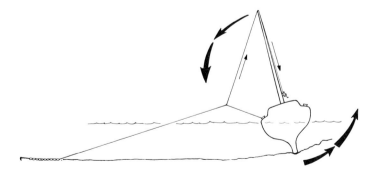

47

halliard on the mast winch the top of the mast is pulled down and the hull turns, reducing the draught. A variant is used on the Ijsselmeer, where going aground is an everyday occurrence. The anchor is laid out into deeper water, and a friend with a motor boat summoned by VHF. The motor boat takes station between the stranded yacht and its anchor and guns engines furiously to make wavelets and lift the canted yacht from the bottom. The latter, when free, winches in its anchor cable until deep water is reached.

Another method is to get a purchase on some fixed object, in this case a mooring buoy. In Fig. 30 the

Fig. 30   Warping-off to buoy — right

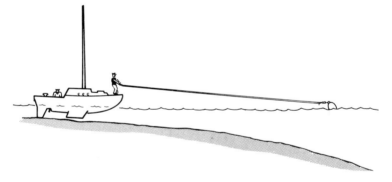

crew of a bilge-keeler that has stranded have run a warp over to a mooring buoy and brought both ends inboard. Weight has been evenly distributed, and the foredeck man is steadily hauling the boat off. In Fig. 31, on the other hand, the crew has not really appreciated that with both of them pulling in the cockpit the underwater profile is acting against them. The skeg remains embedded because the weight of the crew makes it the lowest point.

Fig. 31   Warping-off to buoy — wrong

Kedging-off

The aims of putting out a kedge anchor are first to
provide the kind of leverage that may get the boat off,
and second to make sure things do not get worse. The
sort of worse I have in mind is that species of ill-
considered action that ends up with the boat higher
up the shoal for a much longer time than strictly
necessary. The old Army adage is that reconnaissance
is never wasted, so it is always best to make sure that
the pull the kedge is going to provide will be a pull to
deeper water. When the dinghy is afloat it is worth
sending it off for a few minutes with lead and line, or
sounding pole, to make absolutely sure where the
deepest water may be and where exactly the kedge
should be put down.

The method of doing this must be described, for
many seamanship manuals still tell the reader to carry
out his kedge with the free end of the cable made fast
to the stranded craft. A moment's thought will show
that this cannot be the best way to do it, for if the
object is to get the anchor out as far as possible —

and it is — this is not best accomplished with a loop of cable dangling in the water between boat and dinghy and the weight of it making the task of the rower more difficult. Moreover, the anchor just does not get as far out as it might if used in this way.

Fig. 32   Rowing out the kedge

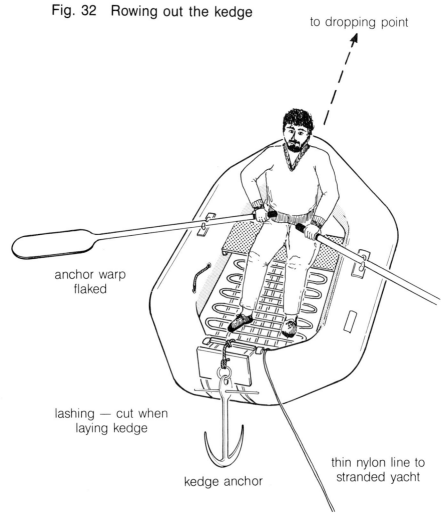

to dropping point

anchor warp
flaked

lashing — cut when
laying kedge

kedge anchor

thin nylon line to
stranded yacht

Figure 32 shows a crewman rowing out a Fisherman anchor ready for dropping as a kedge. The cable is criss-crossed in the bottom of the dinghy for paying out on the way back, and a light nylon line, equivalent in length to the length of the cable, tells him when to cut the lashing and let the kedge fall to the bottom. As kedges are very commonly laid up-wind and up-wave, the crewman can pay out the cable as he drifts back to the grounded yacht, and then pass the bitter end inboard. Those on board can help by pulling him in on the light nylon line and then taking the kedge cable to a winch or cleat. The dinghy should remain in the water in case a second kedge must be laid, and when strain is put on the cable it should be backed by engine, rocking and weight-shifting to give it a fair chance.

Open sea stranding (weather shore, rising tide)

Here the key facts are that deeper water lies down-wind and that more of it will shortly be available. The do's and don'ts are:

Do	*Don't*
Leave the sails up *unless* the direction of the wind in relation to the heading of the boat is such that they will drive it farther on. For example, a close-hauled boat that strands will bump farther on as	Use the anchors initially. With the wind and tide on your side this is no time to interfere with them.
	Send crewmen over the side.

the tide rises. Let the sheets fly and the sails flap free and back the headsail to get the hull moving. One of the crewmen who goes up as part of the weight-shifting process can hold the clew forward into the wind to get the right backward pressure.

Use engine in bursts to coincide with lifting waves.

Stop the engine.

Change the rudder position.

Launch the dinghy straight away; concentrate instead on full astern, rocking, weight-shifting and poling.

Use VHF yet.

Open sea stranding (weather shore, falling tide)

Do

Don't

Launch dinghy. Leave sails up for time being, and follow same procedure as for rising tide. Try to slew boat with head pointing to deeper water.

Use dinghy as an alongside tug — see Fig. 33. Note that it has to be firmly braced with head and stern ropes, plus springs, to be effective, and that the best push

Throw ballast or equipment overboard yet.

Send crewmen into the water without shoes and buoyancy aids. If only one man is to be left on board the remainder should have securing lines round their waists to assist them in re-boarding.

effect is obtained with the dinghy well aft.

Lay out the kedge.

Consider using VHF to summon assistance. Update weather forecast.

Stop the engine until it is certain that the boat is not going to get off.

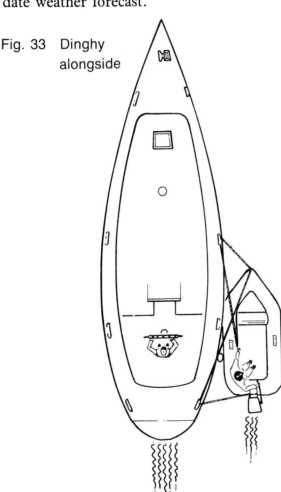

Fig. 33   Dinghy
          alongside

Open sea stranding (lee shore)

With the wind as an enemy, the action of the tide is going to vary from neutral to hostile, and there will be very little difference in what is done with a rising or a falling tide.

Do	*Don't*
Go full astern, stow sails, rock and shift.	Be fearful as you experience sickening crashes in the troughs as the keel or keels slam on the bottom. In general, boats are tougher than crews.
Launch dinghy. Sound if necessary. Put out kedge; make sure the pull is at 180° to the way she went on.	
Get rid of weight in several stages. First, the crew. Then, consider lowering main anchor and cable as a lightening device: if it also takes hold as she bumps along that may be considered a bonus. Fresh water can be pumped out — 75 gallons weighs 750 pounds. Then fuel — 10 litres of diesel weighs 8·7 kilos or 18½ pounds. Ballast and heavy equipment may have to go eventually.	Let the booms swing all over the place — someone may get a nasty crack on the head.
	Let anyone leave the craft without permission and firm instructions, and in particular make sure that the liferaft is not launched without a direct order.
	Allow the crew to become vulnerable through injury or exposure. Insist on full clothing, oilskins, head-gear, shoes or boots and gloves.

Use VHF. Consider the relevance of a "PAN PAN" message if the safety of the ship is at stake. A towing vessel (see p. 50) should be of lesser draught than the stranded one. A vessel with considerable power would be best for making sufficient wash to bounce a boat free.

Towing off by high power (low draught) vessel

Where a boat is likely to pound and suffer hull damage due to the nature of the bottom, it may be an immediate priority to haul it off by brute strength and, perhaps, accept some minor damage now in lieu of major damage later.

In Fig. 34 a yacht has stranded on a rocky beach near high water, and while there are no holes in the

Fig. 34   Towing off by high power (low draught vessel)

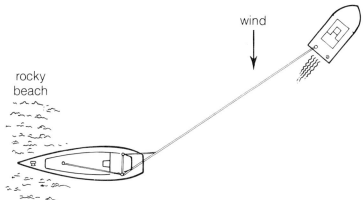

hull at present there may well be if she stays where she is. Her plight has been observed, and a member of the local club offers the services of his powerful and flat-bottomed motor boat. Instant acceptance should be the response, because at the moment the towing craft can come right up to the stern of the yacht, while in an hour or two's time it may not be able to do so. Figure 34 shows the towing boat in a position to best counteract the thrust of the wind and to pull the yacht off as she went on. The craft being towed has not relied merely on cleats to hold the towing line but has fitted a bridle joining two winches so as to spread the load. The towing craft may have to vary the angle of attack to break adhesion in the first instance, pulling at the yacht in the manner of a terrier worrying a bone. It is helpful on such occasions for the two craft to be in touch by VHF or Citizens' Band so that the casualty and the rescuer can exchange information as to which manoeuvres are doing some good and which are counter-productive.

Towing off (vessels of equal draught)

The fundamental problem is often that the towing vessel cannot get close enough to take or pass a line, and three alternatives exist. A towing line, or its messenger, can be thrown, floated across or carried by dinghy. Throwing only works when it is a matter of a few metres, and floating a line down on a lifebuoy or empty water-container depends entirely on wind direction and tidal flow at the time. Usually, the connection must be made by dinghy, and this has the advantage that some of the stranded yacht's gear can be utilized.

Fig. 35 (a) Joining anchor cable and towing warp
(b) Dropping anchor as a kedge

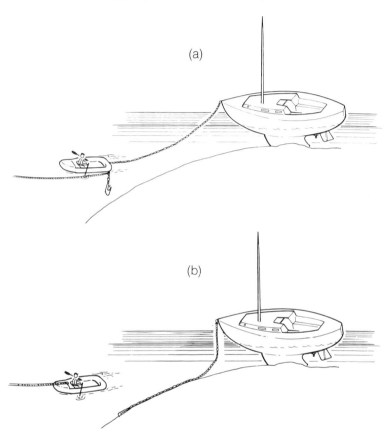

In Fig. 35A a dinghy has been rowed across to a stranded yacht and the anchor cable and towing warp have been joined. Three lines of action may now be followed. First, the towing vessel can use its full strength to attempt to pull the stranded one off the shoal. If that fails, the man in the dinghy can untie the warp and chain and drop the anchor as a kedge — see Fig. 35B. If hauling on the chain results in the stranded yacht coming free, or very nearly free, the man in the dinghy can go back and make the warp fast to the bows of the stranded yacht. A double pull on the towing warp and on the deposited kedge cable should do the trick. The procedure for negotiating a commercial tow-off in a dangerous situation is outlined in the last few pages of this book.

Towing

Where the first line of action just described has succeeded, there is no reason why the gear employed should not also serve as the means of towing a disabled craft to a safe place. In Fig. 36 it may be seen that the anchor half-way down the joined warp and cable is helping to provide the catenary needed to damp down potential stress on the tow-rope. Where the tow is a long one, certain precautions must be taken. The foredeck fittings may not be man enough for the job, and a bridle could be taken right around the cabin top or, in older wooden boats, round the

Fig. 36 Towing with warp and anchor cable

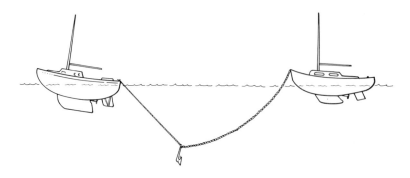

base of the mast. Do not try the latter suggestion with deck-mounted metal masts; they may be damaged by the sudden strains imposed. The guiding principle when towing is to keep a steady pull on the line and avoid "snatching". Course alterations should be wide, shallow turns, and the towed yacht informed by VHF of each change of direction. The towed vessel should always steer precisely in the wake of the towing craft and keep the towline straight. Speed should be kept down — a rough guide is about three knots. When more line is needed it must be paid out slowly to avoid surging. Towing under sail works well when there is a beam wind, although on reaching your destination you must be prepared to reel in the line smartly and turn out of the way of the towed vessel in case, with its residual momentum, it runs into you.

Drying out

The time will come when the water level falls to a point where it is clear to even the most optimistic observer that the boat will not float again this tide. The signs are rigidity in the fore-and-aft axis of the craft, a tendency to list sullenly when rocked, and an end to the grumbling of the keel as it shifts on the bottom and the pounding as it lifts to the waves. From now on, the emphasis has to be on damage limitation, watertight integrity and restricting movement when the tide rises. Centreboarder and bilge-keeler crews will have to put out the right kind of ground tackle and consult the almanac, or use the Twelfths Rule, to find out when their craft are likely to re-float.

That done, it is often a question of waiting it out

and keeping amused. Veterans of the process will
organize cockle-gathering parties, or take the
opportunity to clean the underwater parts of the hull
of weed or slime. It is not unknown for crews of
yachts stranded in, say, the Ray Sand Channel
between the rivers Crouch and Blackwater on the East
Coast, to form cricket teams, have sing-songs and
build sand-castles while waiting for the water to
return.

Boats with more vulnerable underwater profiles will
have to take drying out rather more seriously. The
first priority is to ensure that they dry out "uphill" to
get the best recovery slant for the rising tide; and the
importance of doing so is outlined in Fig. 37. By
drying out "uphill" a 15-degree advantage may be
gained in terms of watertight integrity, for the chief
danger with deep-keel craft is that the incoming tide
floods the hull by way of the cockpit. Smaller ingress
points should not be neglected. All cocks should be

Fig. 37   Downhill and uphill

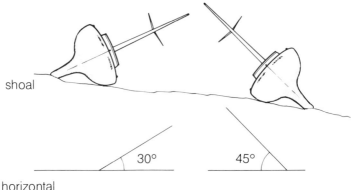

60

turned off, and special care taken to close openings in the hull that are not normally regarded as dangerous. Some types of exhaust, gravity-operated drains and escape holes in calor gas lockers may need to be plugged to keep water out, and where it lips over a cockpit edge a temporary dam of sails, awnings, covers, mattresses and pillows must be hastily erected to maintain watertight integrity during the lifting period. Damage limitation has two components: you must make sure that the hull is protected as it goes down and when it moves about on lift-off.

Protecting the hull

Hull repairs are probably the source of greatest expense to the average boat-owner, and it is wise to sacrifice "soft" equipment to avoid them. As the hull falls on the receding tide, but before it lies supine on its side, some priority must be given to getting padding between the bilge and the sea-bed. In Fig. 38 the crew of a boat drying out on its port bilge have ransacked the cabin and put two bunk mattresses weighed down with a motor-tyre fender and a length of chain in the place where they will do most good. Given the relative costs involved, you should not hesitate to use sails, cushions, bags of clothing, oilskins, bundles of warps or a bagged rubber dinghy under the bilge, weighing them down with chain if necessary to keep them in place. Do not delude yourself that the bottom is soft and no harm will come to an unprotected hull; better to think of sand, shingle or mud as hard, hard, hard.

Immediately before drying out is completed, get into the water again and make a positive check that the padding is in exactly the right place. One or more kedge anchors may already have been laid, but if this is not the case someone will have to splash away to windward with at least two anchors and position them with the wind, or expected wind, bisecting the angle between them — as outlined in the middle drawing of Fig. 23.

Lift-off

The slap of the waves will start to move the boat before she is properly afloat, and after the padding has been recovered it is vital not to try to move too soon. At this stage, everyone should either be on board or in the dinghy, and inlet valves may be opened and blocked openings unblocked. Do not start the engine until quite sure that the little ship has come free, but when clearly afloat it may be used in conjunction with hauling on the anchor cables to work the yacht free.

Fig. 38   Bunk mattresses and fender under drying hull

Where the stranding has taken place near the top of the tide you may need to pivot, shift human weight, heel the boat, hoist sail or call for a wash off or tow to supplement engine and anchors.

Lights, shapes, flags and signals

A stranded vessel has obligations to other boats and ships in her vicinity, and these obligations may begin *before* the stranding takes place. A yacht being blown ashore by stress of weather, or after the failure of ground tackle, should fly in her crosstrees the International Code of Signals flag "Y". This single-letter urgent signal means: I AM DRAGGING MY ANCHOR, and has the dual purpose of telling other craft that you are in some specific difficulty, while the red and yellow diagonal striped flag also warns them that there is a danger of the dragging craft fouling the cables of others anchored in her path.

Fig. 39   Aground by day in fog

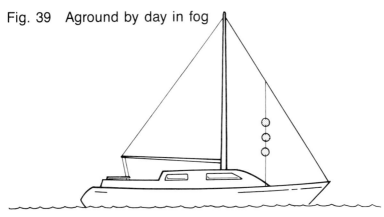

Bell: ding-ding-ding — rapid ringing — ding-ding-ding
Horn: short — prolonged — short

A yacht of less than 12 metres in length is not formally required to show the lights and shapes laid down in the Collision Regulations for a vessel aground but it may, and those over 12 metres must, display three balls in a vertical line by day — see Fig. 39. At night, the grounded vessel shows two all-round red lights disposed vertically together with the single white all-round anchor light. In fog or restricted visibility the sound signal for a stranded yacht over 12 metres long is a rapid ringing of a bell for about five seconds at intervals of not more than one minute, preceded and followed by three distinct strokes of the bell. The bell signal, in Morse terms, is S – T – S and manifestly derives from S – O – S. The horn signal is the letter "R" — just the same as that for a vessel at anchor — and these signals are given in word form with Fig. 39. Yachts under 12 metres long that do not make these signals may make some other effective sound at intervals of not more than two minutes. I would suggest that a frying-pan used as a gong, or a whistle, might make useful substitutes when there are no bells or horns on board.

If your plight is observed you may see three white star rockets fired ashore, and the meaning is: YOU ARE SEEN: HELP WILL BE GIVEN AS SOON AS POSSIBLE. Additionally, the Coast Guard or harbour authority may send a VHF message to this effect. The transmission of a "SECURITAY" or "PAN PAN" message by you is a matter of judgement, and the first consideration must be that "SECURITAY" conveys a navigational warning, while "PAN PAN" indicates that the safety of the ship is at stake, while danger is not imminent and immediate assistance is not required. In particular, the use of an urgency signal will depend very much on future weather, hull integrity, means of propulsion and crew morale. A "MAYDAY" message is not at all ambiguous. It says to all the world that the vessel transmitting it is threatened by grave and imminent danger and requests immediate assistance. The flag signals relating to stranding are equally clear. The two-flag signal "JH" means: I AM AGROUND; I AM NOT IN DANGER, while "JG" signifies: I AM AGROUND; I AM IN A DANGEROUS SITUATION. Should a would-be rescuer venture too close you can warn him off by either "JL": YOU ARE RUNNING THE RISK OF GOING AGROUND, or the simpler single-flag "U" meaning: YOU ARE STANDING INTO DANGER. A vessel coming off the ground and following an erratic course in crowded waters could always signal by single flag or Morse the letter "D": KEEP CLEAR OF ME — I AM MANOEUVRING WITH DIFFICULTY.

Long-term stranding

Where a boat has stranded at or near High Water Springs, or has been carried by wave action well up the beach, it will often be necessary to use exceptional remedies. These may be summarized under digging out, shoring up, lifting, lightening, and pushing and pulling.

Digging out

There is nothing more infuriating than finding out that the stranded craft floats upright at high water but does not break free because ridges of sand or mud have formed along the keel. In calm and secure conditions the cure is to take a couple of shovels down at low water and dig a trench on both sides of the keel with a lead to deeper water. Anchors and warps need to be bar-taut for this procedure to work properly, because all the labour will be wasted if the boat floats askew and breaks down the edges of the excavation. In Fig. 40 the trench dug under the keel continues seawards for a respectable distance, while the warps and cables are kept tight until the vessel floats. Thereafter, it is a matter of slackening carefully from the stern and hauling slowly from the bow to stay straight until deep water is reached. A boat that has been washed up above high water mark may have to be dug out by a bucket crane, bulldozer or JCB, and it may be best to make the trench on the downhill side of the hull, just clear of the keel, and allow the rising water to crumble the sides, pulling the boat broadside into the trench to get it upright.

Fig. 40   Digging a trench along the keel

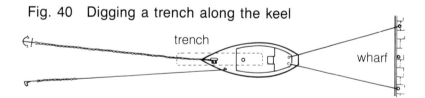

Shoring up

Racing craft with deep keels are particularly liable to be damaged when stranded, and consideration should be given to supporting them on makeshift legs. In general, spinnaker booms and tubular alloy spars are just not strong enough to hold up heavy displacement craft, and pieces of substantial timber have to be used. Figure 41A shows what can be done in an emergency. Three heavy timber spars have been obtained, and

Fig. 41   Shoring up — makeshift legs

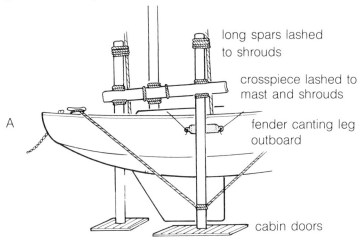

A

long spars lashed
to shrouds

crosspiece lashed to
mast and shrouds

fender canting leg
outboard

cabin doors

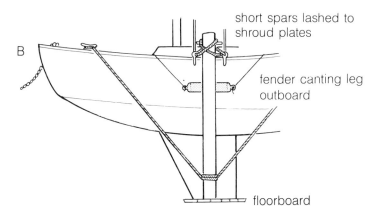

B

short spars lashed to
shroud plates

fender canting leg
outboard

floorboard

two of them have been lashed to the shrouds with a
third as a cross-piece. The cabin doors have been
unshipped and used as ground-plates to take the
thrust, while the whole structure is stiffened by
lashing the cross-piece to the mast and fixing fore-and-
aft guys to prevent buckling. In Fig. 41B the

resourceful crew have obtained some clothes' posts from shore and tied them to the shroud plates, using floorboards as ground plates. In both drawings, the essential outward thrust of the legs has been achieved by putting fenders between the supporting posts and the hulls.

Lifting

This can be considered under three headings: lifting by means of air-filled containers, by ground-based machines and by helicopter. The use of air-bags, drums or barrels may have to be contemplated when the viscous nature of the bottom is such that the boat does not come unstuck even though the water level is right. The usual method is to pass ropes or wires under the hull, attach the air containers as low down as possible at low tide and then inflate using an air hose and a compressor. The hose will also be used to blast out tunnels under the keel to pass the lifting material through, and in at least one instance that I know of the lift was successful with a dozen of the largest sized inflatable fenders.

Where small craft end up high and dry it is often easier to recover them from the land side, using a mobile crane or portable derrick to lift them on to a trailer and thence away by road. Finally, there is the lift by helicopter — particularly appropriate when the boat is stranded on an isolated rock or at the foot of steep cliffs. The assent of your insurance company will invariably be required, but it is worth recording that in 1987 a Chinook helicopter lifted a stranded cruiser from Kimmeridge Ledges after it had broken adrift from its moorings. In a classic no-blame situation like this, the insurance company will weigh up the cost of salvage and the cost of paying up on a policy and make the decision for you.

Lightning

In many stranding cases it is merely a matter of raising the hull six or seven centimetres to unstick it from the ground, and we have already noted the benefits gained from removing those weighty but portable objects — people. Kedging takes a man, an anchor and chain, an outboard and a tank of fuel off the yacht. The next logical candidates are cooking-gas bottles, tins of fuel and oil, and those very heavy navigational aids, books. Spare clothing, cases of food and toolkits can be ferried ashore and, as a last resort, the fresh water and fuel can be pumped overboard, although it would be prudent to retain enough of the latter to engine the little ship out of danger — while the locals will not thank you for polluting their favourite bathing beach. One obvious method, often forgotten during the bustle, is to pump the bilges dry, while ballast can come out *provided* a note is made of where it is cached and how it fits back in. A cooker weighs 33 kilograms, a marine toilet 27 kilograms and a six-man liferaft upwards of 45 kilograms. When a boat is emptied of gear each winter the hull rises several centimetres out of the water: translate that rise to the stranding situation and you will appreciate how much can be done by simple lightening.

Pulling and pushing

Leverage can be obtained from a variety of objects if your boat is stranded reasonably close to the shore.

For example, in Fig. 42 a heavy displacement motor boat has gone aground just outside the harbour wall. The owner has run a line ashore and taken it through a block tied to a bollard. A friend, summoned by radio, has brought his pick-up truck and is slowly easing the boat off the shoal. A well-fendered power boat can act as a pusher tug while another tows, and steel boats may be shoved up or down a beach by a JCB with rollers brought up and removed every few metres or so.

At the low technology end of the spectrum lies people power, and it is a potential asset not to be despised. Once, aground off Clacton Pier during a

Fig. 42 Pulling off by pick-up truck

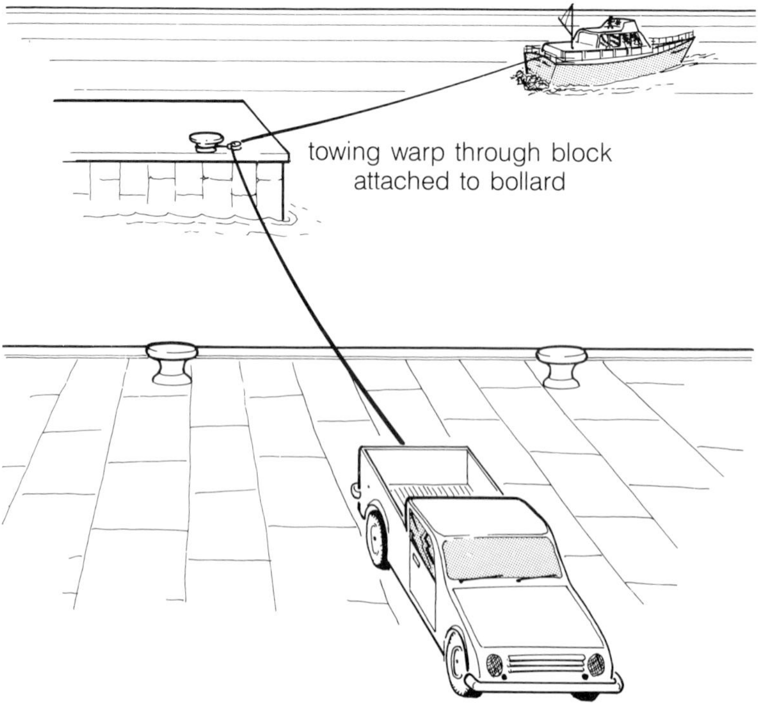

towing warp through block
attached to bollard

Bank Holiday, a friend of mine swam ashore and
mustered fifty bathers. He disposed them evenly and,
at a given signal, they heaved in unison and swung
the bows seawards. At a second command, and amid a
mighty cheer, they pushed manfully and propelled the
yacht safely back into deep water.

Beaching and scuttling

Deliberate beaching may sometimes be justified when,
for example, a holed boat is sinking rapidly or a
crewman is so badly injured that this is the quickest
and surest way of saving life; but the general rule
must be: don't do it. The reason is that boats beached
on purpose in any kind of weather are almost
invariably damaged, while those beached in face of
bad weather are often lost. The practice of scuttling
seems to be confined to hurricane areas, notably the
West Indies and the Pacific, and the reasoning behind
it is that it is better for the interior to be water-
damaged than that the whole be knocked to bits. The
problem of hurricane-force winds arises but rarely in
European waters, and scuttling would be a difficult
tactic to defend when establishing an insurance claim.
As will emerge in the last part of this book, the duty
of an owner is not only to struggle against the perils
of the sea and protect his property, but also to be
seen to do so.

Wreck

Precautions beforehand

Being wrecked is a traumatic business for which no one is ever fully mentally prepared. The precautions that everyone can take beforehand, however, will do much to rob shipwreck of its worst physical terrors and minimize the risk to life. Being prepared in three areas — information, the panic bag and the liferaft — is central to survival.

Information

The rescue services often have the gravest difficulty in sorting out which craft is in trouble from the relatively large number sailing near the coast in the summer months, and it is vital that your yacht bears a name, number or identification sign that can be seen from the sea and from the air. The name should be prominently displayed on the topsides, cockpit dodgers or wheelhouse, for most inscriptions on either bow or at the stern are not visible at a distance in any kind of sea. Similarly, a class letter and number, racing number or fishing letters and numbers ought to be shown either on deck or, better still, in the upper part of the mainsail where no amount of reefing will obscure it.

The value of such information is enormously enhanced if the boat owner is a member of the Yacht and Boat Safety Scheme and has filled in Form CG66. A copy of this form is reproduced as Fig. 43, and it may be seen that the Coastguard, who co-ordinate most rescues, will be able to reconcile information from two sources and take decisions accordingly. Even the knowledge that the craft is rigged, or has no

Fig. 43 Yacht and Boat Safety Scheme — data

DEPARTMENT OF TRANSPORT
HM COASTGUARD
YACHT AND BOAT SAFETY SCHEME

M336

Name of Craft

How and where is the name displayed

Type of Craft — Type of rig

Sailing or fishing number

Colours of craft — Speed and endurance under power

Hull above water / below water — Details of radio

Superstructure — HF MF Trans/Rec:

Sail — VHF Channels and call sign:

Spinnaker — Other Equipment:

Length ____ feet ____ metres

Details of any special identification features — Type of distress signals carried

Details of Owner
Name
Address

Tel. No
Signature
Date

Details of Shore Contact
Name
Address

Usual base — Dinghy type

Usual mooring — colour

Tel. No. — Life raft type

Usual activity (eg fishing, racing, etc). — serial no.

Name of Club or Association

Usual sea areas — Are life jackets carried

Form CG66

tophamper to speak of, will be valuable to rescuers, while type and colour of dinghy, make of liferaft and hull colour will be important recognition and action data.

The panic bag

Every yacht that ventures beyond a 30-kilometre radius from its home base should carry a portable container to hold essential items if a swift departure from the boat is called for. This container should be waterproof, reasonably resistant to fire, be fitted with a carrying strap and sufficiently compact to be carried one-handed and thrown across a gap between boats moving up and down in a swell. The basic contents are listed first, and are chosen to combat equally the perils of bureaucracy and those of a remote shore.

Essential contents of panic bag

Passports; ship registration papers; paper money.
Cheques and cards; address book; small change
    for telephone.
First aid kit; sunglasses, toothbrush, knife.
Pocket torch, flare, tin of matches, Horlicks
    tablets.

Optional extras

Fork, spoon and cup; fish hooks, polythene bottle
    of water.
Towel, linen hat. Spare sweater; spare socks.

As may be seen, the contents of the panic bag will suffice for merely a few hours ashore providing, as they do, the materials for a hot drink, a partial change into dry clothing, some sun protection, minimum medical care and, in a civilized milieu, the means of getting the crew to their homes. In the longer run, it is the liferaft that will carry the larger range of useful equipment.

Liferafts

Your liferaft should be serviced annually, be readily accessible above decks in a durable, weatherproof container, and lightly, but firmly, fastened. It is no good having a liferaft so securely lashed down that it cannot be released in 30 seconds or so, and ideally speaking it should be attached to the parent craft at just three points — as in Fig. 44. This illustration shows a raft in a fibreglass container secured by two broad straps to a deck mounting and having the opening cord tied to the handrail. Thus, the launching

Fig. 44   Liferaft in glassfibre container for deck stowage

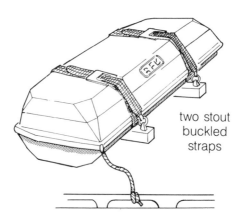

two stout
buckled
straps

of the raft is accomplished by undoing the two buckled straps and throwing the container bodily overboard. When it reaches the full limit of the opening cord a tug on the cord will actuate the CO_2 cylinder and ensure inflation. The equipment your liferaft should carry comes under two headings.

Essential liferaft equipment

Rescue line	Repair outfit	Two sponges
Two paddles	Drinking vessel	Pump
First Aid kit	60 anti-seasick	Torch
Two distress rockets	tablets	Instruction leaflet
Rescue signal table	Drogue	Two tin-openers
Three flares	Drinking water (half	
Safety knife	a litre per head)	

Fig. 45   Liferaft in valise

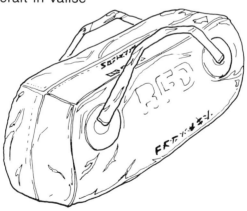

Additional liferaft equipment

Tinned and dried	Clothing	Ocean charts
food	Fishing gear	Extra water
Solar still		

An EPIRB (Emergency Position Indicating Radio Beacon)

77

Valise liferafts are on the market (see Fig. 45), but it is only proper to say that they are a slightly inferior product from the safety point of view. There is a tendency to stow them low down in a deep locker where they are difficult to fish out in an emergency, and the operating cord has to be made fast to a strongpoint before throwing the valise overboard. Additionally, there is the psychological disincentive that as they are not on display and must be brought out for use a skipper with other problems on his mind will delay the launch of the raft. All in all, there is a lot to be said for having the liferaft deck-mounted, visible and available for immediate employment.

Yacht safety equipment

The panic bag and liferaft contents may be supplemented by safety equipment routinely carried on the parent craft. This should consist of:

A BSI-standard lifejacket or buoyancy aid for every person on board.

A safety harness for every person on board.

Two lifebuoys — one with a self-igniting light and the other having a self-activating smoke float.

Types of wreck

There seems to be four categories of dangerous stranding leading to shipwreck, and they are: the blown-ashore or stress of weather type; fog-induced strandings; navigational error; and failure of anchor or cable. Peter Tangvald has worked out that one in five casualties are due to the failure of ground tackle, and it appears reasonable that the fog-induced and navigational error categories account for most of the rest, as the blown-ashore wreck is, in most years, a small percentage of the whole in western Europe. A sizeable sub-category of navigational error may be noted: racing yachts tend to hug the shore to cheat the tide and reduce distance run, and these strandings may be put down as the triumph of optimism over experience. Fortunately, most of the mistakes made when racing are in sheltered waters with rescue and escort craft in close attendance.

Initial impact procedure

A dangerous stranding of the sort that leads to wreck often occurs at night and in heavy seas. The ordinary noises of a boat under way are increased fivefold by the crunching of the keel on the bottom, the thump of waves on the topsides and the increase in wind that always seems to come at such moments. Further confusion results from the violent displacement of objects that destroys the familiarity of the cabin, and the awkward grounding angle that makes movement difficult. Some crew members may be half-dressed; some shouting and others rigid with fright or red-faced with anger. There is a tendency to do things without orders; to cast off this and that without thought and pay excessive attention to the engine or sails when it is quite apparent that no amount of tweaking or manoeuvring will be of any use as things stand. The old sea adage, culled and bowdlerized from the Collision Regulations, should come to mind, so that the rule is:

> When in danger, or in doubt,
> Don't wave your arms, or run about!

while the first order to be given is that everyone gets fully dressed, puts on footwear and dons buoyancy aids or lifejackets. Too many clothes are better than too few, and everyone must have a knife, put on a hat and wear gloves. The skipper can set a good example by remaining calm, concentrating on motivating others and refraining from shouting, cursing or wrenching at various bits of gear.

The second step is to find out if watertight integrity has been breached, for the answer makes all the difference as to what happens next. Instruct the crew to pull up floorboards, open lockers and peer into the bilges to see what level of water lies beneath. Taste it, if necessary, to find out if it is just the usual mixture of fuel, oil and ullage that swishes around in most hulls, or is fresh (denoting perhaps a leak of drinking water), mostly fuel (indicating a ruptured tank or broken pipe), or warm (sign of a displaced pipe from the engine cooling system). The worst news of all will be finding a quantity of cold, salt water and perhaps hearing more of the same entering the hull. Do not automatically assume that all is lost and proceed to abandon ship, for many hulls have what might be called a bilge magnification factor that makes things look worse than they are. In one yacht of my acquaintance there is so little space for bilge water under the floorboards that the pockets of coats hanging in a locker are permanently sopping wet because a few gallons lick up the inside of the hull when going to windward, and the same angle may be present when aground. The sound of water entering under pressure may also damage morale but, as explained later, abandonment should not be considered until a quite specific level has been reached. For the time being, let us assume that there are no holes in the hull and look at what follows.

Sound hull

Unless the weather is so bad as to make on-deck activity highly dangerous, the prudent skipper will carry out the procedures set out for a stranding in the central part of this book, with two amendments. He will assess how the boat is stuck and on what type of bottom. He will consider what the sails can do, and if the engine can help. Weight-shifting, poling, "sugging", canting, kedging and lightening may all be tried, but two additional lines of action must be in his mind. He should think about sending what might be called the non-combatants ashore — typically, older crewmen and children whose weight is not compensated for by their physical strength — and use of VHF radio. The actual circumstances will dictate the type of message sent. With a sound hull and the safety of the ship at stake, but no imminent danger and need for immediate assistance, it appears that a "PAN PAN" message is the most appropriate.

Holed hull

The two priorities are to stop more water getting in and to pump out what is already there. Anyone who has tried to staunch an inflow of water will know that the laws of physics are acting against them, and that filling a hole from the inside only works successfully when the leak is at or near the waterline. Planking can be levered back into place, and a ragged tear in fibreglass may be temporarily plugged by a sail bag, pillow or bundle of clothing, but the long-term solution is to cover the hole from the outside before filling it.

The quickest method is to try fothering — as shown in Fig. 46. A sail, preferably a thick one like a storm jib, is secured with a rope under the hull and, when all is taut, soft material is pushed between hull and sail to reduce water inflow to a dribble. Foam mattress filling is ideal, and layers of canvas from a cover build up progressively to keep water at bay. At this stage you will be beyond caring about the appearance of the boat, and it may be helpful to use oil to calm the waves and reduce the thrust of the sea. Diesel and paraffin are fairly useless, being too light

Fig. 46 Fothering a leak

for the purpose, but lubricating oil — especially used engine oil — can have a spectacular smoothing effect. Dangle the tin or tins over the side to windward, having first punched a small hole near the bottom with the spike on your knife. The resulting film of oil will spread round the boat and up to windward, and will greatly assist the successful launching of dinghy and liferaft at a later stage.

Pumping and bailing may have to be continuous, and it is worth considering three means of supplementing the normal work of bilge pumps. With the engine running, it is possible to close the water inlet cock, disconnect the hose and let it dangle into the bilges to pump out through the engine exhaust. The toilet pump can be pressed into service by a similar disconnection, and where a hole is amidships and there is a cockpit fitted with drains it may be possible to pour water out of the cabin and dispose of it through the cockpit. Finally, there is the chain of buckets passing water aft to tip out over the side or up through a fo'c'sle hatch. As the saying goes, no pump is half as effective as a frightened man with a pail in his hands.

Signals of distress

There are many varieties of signal, and what follows is an attempt to grade them in a roughly ascending order of urgency and to comment on the usefulness of each one.

Signal	Comment
1 Raising and lowering extended arms.	See Fig. 47. Effective by day in well-frequented waters. It is, in

effect, a private distress signal to craft in the immediate vicinity, and is particularly useful when seeking a tow off or the removal of surplus personnel.

2 A *distant signal*, consisting of a square flag with a ball hoisted beneath it.

The upside-down ensign conveys the same sort of message — that assistance is required.

3 International Code flags "NC", with the "N" over the "C".

Similarly, the International Code flag "V", or the Morse Code signal · · · —, means: I REQUIRE ASSISTANCE.

Fig. 47 Distress signal: vertical movement of extended arms

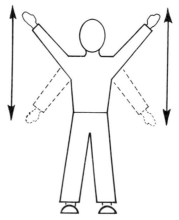

4 A continuous sounding with any form of signalling apparatus.

The Department of Trade prefers that "SOS" (· · · — — — · · ·) is sounded. At night, flashing "SOS" by torch *towards* a potential recipient (lighthouse, coastguard station or other vessels) may work well.

5 A gun or other explosive signal fired at intervals of about a minute.

Chiefly for big ships, but useful when stranded in fog.

6 Orange smoke.

By day, using hand-held smoke candles.

7 Flames on the vessel.

Be careful. Burning oily rags in a bucket hoisted outboard on a boathook is probably the safest method. Not much good in the southern North Sea where incinerator ships operate.

8 Rockets throwing out red stars.

Best set off in pairs, with the first one attracting attention and the second giving the bearing.

9 Red parachute flares, or a hand-held red flare.

Fire the Very pistol vertically *unless* low cloud will obscure the signal. Hand-held red flares to be directed down-wind to avoid burns from sparks. Use white flares later to show rescuers your exact position.

10 Radio signals. Four possibilities. "SOS" by Morse Code, and auto-alarm signals. An EPIRB which transmits for 48 hours and acts as a homing device, and "MAYDAY" by VHF.

"MAYDAY" signals are best for small yachts, and the form a message should take is: MAYDAY — MAYDAY — MAYDAY. THIS IS YACHT HOPEFULLY — YACHT HOPEFULLY — YACHT HOPEFULLY. MAYDAY. YACHT HOPEFULLY. ONE SIX ZERO TWO HUNDRED METRES FROM HENGISTBURY HEAD. STRUCK BEERPAN ROCKS. DISABLED AND HOLED. REQUIRE IMMEDIATE ASSISTANCE. TOTAL CREW FOUR ON WHITE SLOOP. OVER.

To which may be added, for very small craft, the waving of clothing tied to an oar and a rapid raising and lowering of sails to attract attention. It must be emphasized that distress signals must not be made unless serious or imminent danger is anticipated, and that the sending of a distress signal may only be authorized by the skipper.

Replies to distress signals

Two kinds of response may be made. The initial response to a "MAYDAY" call may be in the following terms.

MAYDAY — YACHT HOPEFULLY — HOPEFULLY — HOPEFULLY. THIS IS YACHT SPEEDY — SPEEDY — SPEEDY. RECEIVED — MAYDAY.

Where shore-based authorities have had a visual sighting of your distress signal and wish to indicate that your plight has been observed they may either:

1 Set off an orange smoke signal.
2 Fire three Thunderlights at one-minute intervals.
3 Or, at night, fire three white star signals at one-minute intervals.

The decision to abandon

The saving of life must take absolute precedence over any property considerations, and in some strandings it will be apparent early on that wreck cannot be avoided. A boat piled up on a rocky lee shore with the waves already too high for dinghy work and with a gale forecast, should be abandoned *before* the weather deteriorates. No question of courage, or lack of it, arises, for life saving comes first and in the act of abandonment certain action can be taken that may limit damage. Securing lines can be taken ashore; the lightening of the craft may enable it to float higher up the beach and professional salvage help may be summoned.

Leaving the yacht in good order by dinghy or liferaft is better than leaving it so late that some crew will have to swim ashore. Where this latter option is unavoidable, make sure that fenders or some other floating objects secured to warps are put over the side to give swimmers a chance of having something to hang on to for part of the way to the beach. The moment to abandon a holed boat can be precisely stated. When the water reaches the wedding tackle of a man standing in the main cabin it is time to go. The decision to abandon must be made, and clearly announced, by the skipper.

Abandon ship procedure

No craft should be abandoned before rockets and flares have been set off; before a "MAYDAY" signal saying exactly where the wreck has taken place, and its cause, has been transmitted; and before the panic bag has been put in the dinghy or raft. Launch the liferaft by throwing it overboard to leeward and well clear of the wreck and, when it is at the extremity of the opening cord (about 25 metres), pull sharply to get inflation from the CO_2 bottle. *Do not untie or cut the opening cord yet.* In about 30 seconds the raft will have sufficient buoyancy to bear weight. Discourage crewmen from jumping on to the canopy; it is usually best to haul in on the opening cord so that boarding may take place close under the lee of the parent craft with crewmen getting into the raft with one foot on the gas bottle/step (shown at "B" in Fig. 48) and hands grasping the handles at "A" in the same illustration. Although everyone should be carrying a knife, no one should cut the cord without a specific order. After all, you may wish to stand by the parent craft for some time, or even climb back in to get food or water, charts or sleeping bags. Confiscate sharp objects, such as belt buckles or nailed shoes, that may pierce the fabric, and close the canopy opening as far as possible to maintain body warmth and combat the wind chill factor. Tie dinghy and liferaft firmly together where both have been launched, and consider your next move with some care. If out of sight of land, and in darkness, it might be politic to remain near the wreck and wait for daylight. With a beach downwind and a regular sea running in without a display of breaking crests or cross-swell, it could be advantageous to cut the securing cord and make for land.

Conduct in the raft

Extreme instability is a characteristic of liferafts, and it will do no harm to issue seasickness tablets right away. Normally, there should be no issue of food and water during the first few hours until occupants are used to the motion, for vomiting is both debilitating and wasteful of scarce resources.

Take firm charge, ordering one person to keep a look-out through a crack in the canopy opening,

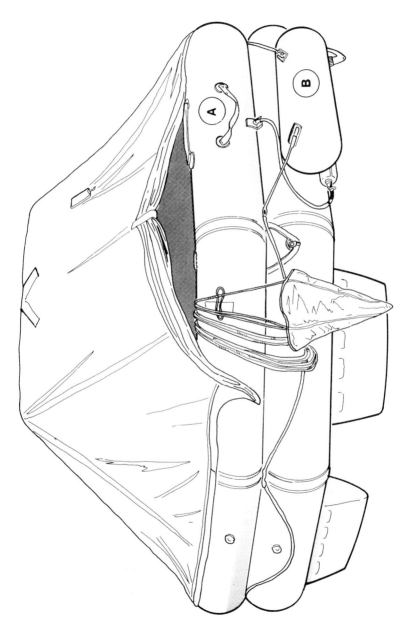

Fig. 48   Boarding the liferaft: handles at "A", step at "B"

another to bail and a third to mop up the last of the wetness with a sponge. It will hardly be necessary to order that the crew huddle together for warmth; the interior dimensions are such that a collective heat balance will soon be achieved. Speak cheerfully and emphasize the likelihood of an early rescue or arrival on firm ground, and give such first aid as space permits. Usually this will amount to little more than sticking on plasters, bandaging and bathing cuts and bruises with salt water. Top up the buoyancy chambers at fixed intervals, and establish some kind of watch system. Liferafts with inflatable floors are best kept well pumped up to improve insulation.

In the longer term, it may be necessary to rig a sea anchor in order to remain near the wreck scene, work out a food scale, start collecting rainwater, set up a solar still and begin calculating the rate and set of drift. A log should be started, with a record of those aboard as the first entry. Quite soon, in a remote sea area, it will be necessary to think about supplementing supplies with fish from the sea or birds from the air.

Rescue

There are four possibilities to consider. Rescue may come by means of helicopter, from lifeboats, by coastguard apparatus or by own efforts, and I will deal with each in turn.

Helicopter

Pilots are always nervous of getting the winch cable tangled with the masts and rigging of a sailing craft, and pick-ups are best made from a liferaft or dinghy held reasonably stationary and at a respectable distance from a wreck. The most useful thing that you can do when the helicopter is close by is to set off an orange smoke signal to indicate your whereabouts and give the wind direction. Do *not* fire rockets or flares at, or near, hovering helicopters. The crew may hold up printed notices telling you, for example, to jump into the water one at a time for pick-up, or the winchman may come down on the cable and shout directions. If the winchline, or its rope messenger, are passed down do *not* make it fast to any part of the boat, raft or dinghy.

Survivors in the water will be recovered by a strop if they can help themselves, and be put into it by a helicopter crewman if they are numb with cold or stiffened by exposure. In the case of motor yachts with little tophamper, the lifting of survivors may be accomplished from the upper deck, and it will help rescuers a great deal if a big "H" is painted on a clear piece of deck, preferably near the stern if wind and wave have swivelled the wreck head to weather. Remember that helicopters will not operate at night, in reduced visibility or in winds of over 45 knots. Rescue helicopters are fitted with marine VHF sets, and usually use Channel 6.

Lifeboat

The inshore rescue craft, with its shallow draught and high speed, is much more likely to come alongside a wreck to take you off than its larger cousin; while the deep-water lifeboat may, if the coxswain thinks it advisable, take you in tow or try a pluck-off. Both types will take survivors from a raft, and it is only very occasionally that there is any question of salvage. In the *Viscount* case of 1966 a vessel towed into port by the Cromer lifeboat after being aground in fog was subject to such a claim, but so few claims are made by lifeboatmen that it need hardly be a consideration. Salvage will be dealt with later, but I believe that a substantial contribution to the RNLI box, hearty thanks and a few pints all round squares accounts. The only thing that upsets lifeboatmen is the call-out where no danger exists, and I treasure the memory of a cartoon reproduced in a yachting magazine many years ago. Two lifeboatmen are leaning on the rail of their craft, with a jaunty yacht nodding gently to the swell in the background. The first lifeboatman is commenting sourly to his companion: "Gent says 'ee's got electronic failure: can 'ee 'ave a tow . . .?"

Coastguard rescue equipment

A boat that sets off distress signals when aground in a dangerous position under steep cliffs may bring to the scene a contingent of Coastguards with breeches-buoy and rocket life-saving apparatus. After setting up, they will fire a rocket over the craft with an 8-millimetre hemp line attached. Once you have hold of this line make an affirmative sign — as in Fig. 50. A tailed block with an endless fall rove through it will be attached, and when the same affirmative signal is made on shore you may haul in. The block has a rope called the jackstay running from it, and an end that secures to part of the yacht — often the mast. When made fast, cast off the rocket line and make the affirmative signal again. The Coastguards will tighten the jackstay from their end and make it fast.

Fig. 49   Coastguard rescue equipment

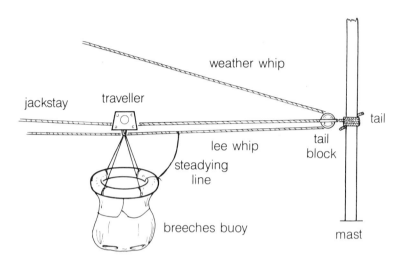

The breeches buoy is pulled out to you on the endless fall and suspended from the jackstay on a travelling block — as in Fig. 49. Instruct your crewmen that they are to get inside the breeches buoy, taking the weight on their elbows and facing towards the shore so that they can use their feet when pulled over rocks or up the cliff-face. The affirmative signal is again given as a sign that the shore party may begin pulling, and the negative signal (shown in Fig. 51) is made to indicate "stop". Tension and the angle of pull often require adjustment, and most Coastguard units have VHF radio and will use Channel 16 to communicate with the wreck. In some cases, lighter equipment consisting of an inflatable lifejacket in place of the breeches buoy will be employed, and a harness must be buckled on. Instructions are printed on the lifejacket.

Own efforts

One of the advantages of inflating and launching the dinghy in addition to the liferaft is that you then have the means of towing, or at least guiding the drift of, the latter and can pick out the best landing place. Further, while there is a chance of refloating the yacht you have the means of getting off to it again in calm weather and trying some of the options discussed in the central part of this book. You are better placed, with a dinghy, to police the wreck and salvage personal property, in addition to saving two expensive items of equipment.

Liferafts are often destroyed by rescuers to avoid misleading those who voyage that way later on, and with the 1988 combined price for a dinghy and liferaft working out at about £1,500 the insurers will be pleased that you have behaved in this responsible way. Getting ashore in this dinghy/liferaft combination can be tricky with a heavy sea, and signals from the shore will be of the greatest help. In Fig. 50 a helper on

Fig. 50   Signal: "This is the best place to land"

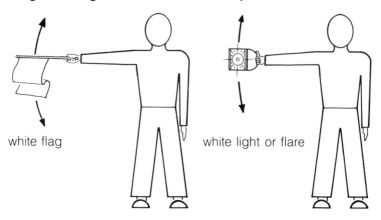

white flag

white light or flare

shore is signalling that where he stands is the best place to land. In Fig. 51 the "wave-off" motions across the body signify that landing is highly dangerous where the man is standing. However, there

Fig. 51 Signal: "Landing here highly dangerous"

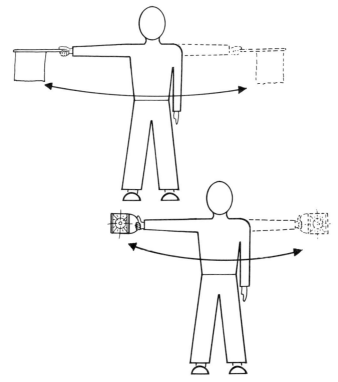

is a safer place near at hand, and in Fig. 52 the person signalling from the shore has left one of his flags or lights at the dangerous point and is walking away with the other. When he stops and makes the "best place to land" signal shown in Fig. 50 you will be able to paddle in through the surf with some confidence.

Fig. 52   Signal: "Go in direction indicated"

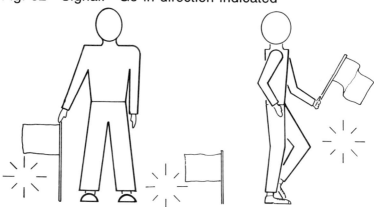

The hostile shore

For the most part, readers of this book who are
shipwrecked will land at a fertile and inhabited shore,
but it will do no harm to put in here a condensed
guide to survival on a hostile and empty sea-coast.

The rules for eating and drinking are simple.
Rainwater, and that issuing from rocks, is usually
pure, and water from pits dug in the ground is
generally so, provided that man, the arch-polluter, is
absent. If in doubt, boil all water for three minutes
before drinking. Salt-water fish fresh from the sea
may be eaten raw; fresh-water fish should be cooked.
All land mammals and birds are edible after their
intestines and reproductive tracts have been removed.
All plants and their fruits, seeds, bark, tubers, buds,
flowers, nuts, stems and roots are worth nibbling at:
reject only those with milky sap or a bitter taste.
Avoid caterpillars, spiny and inflatable fish, unboiled
crustaceans and highly coloured fungi. If in doubt, see
what rodents, pigeons or parrots eat, for what is good
for them is good for you.

Legal problems

The law of salvage is finely balanced to take account of the interests of the owners of a vessel, the insurers and the salvagers, and the basic principle is that of "no cure, no pay". Consequently, when your boat is obviously going to be knocked to pieces if nothing is done, it is in everybody's interests to enlist the services of others under a "no cure, no pay" contract on the grounds that it is better that something be saved rather than everything be lost. The time-hallowed form of contract for salvage is set out in a document called Lloyds Open Form, and a short version appears in Fig. 53. Sometimes, it is not physically possible to get signatures on paper because the boats cannot get alongside each other, but shouted consent across the wave-tops, or even a verbal agreement made over the VHF, will be good enough to clinch the deal. The salvagers' reward will be determined later by reference to the value of the salvaged property and the risks taken during a specific period of time. Most problems arise when what is asked for, or done, falls short of full salvage, and typically when a tow-off is negotiated.

Tow-off procedure

A stranded vessel that, in the opinion of the skipper, is not necessarily going to become a wreck, can be towed off the ground at a fee agreed with the person in charge of the towing craft. When making such an agreement it is essential to:

(a) agree an inclusive price for the service beforehand;

97

(b) use your own towing lines or warps;

(c) prevent personnel from the towing craft boarding you, or bringing any gear over from their boat;

(d) make a note of the weather, sea state, witnesses to the agreement, the exact terms of the bargain and the method to be used.

Do not:

(e) disclose the value of your boat;

(f) indicate that it is insured;

(g) leave your vessel.

If, as it turns out, you have to use equipment supplied by the towing craft, fix a price for the service. Make your offer sufficiently generous to obviate subsequent grumbling, but not so absurdly generous as to arouse cupidity. Fishermen, in particular, will have a very good idea of what their time and labour is worth, so it is best to pitch your first offer at a reasonable level and pay up promptly when the job is done.

Wreck ownership

The ownership of wreck-associated property is a little complicated. Jetsam (property thrown overboard to lighten ship); lagan (property thrown overboard but marked or buoyed to aid subsequent recovery); and flotsam (property found floating about with no clue as to how it got there) all belong to the first finder *unless* an owner can be traced. Unclaimed property on the shore belongs to the Receiver of Wrecks, although the

Fig. 53   Simple Form of Salvage Agreement

SIMPLE FORM OF SALVAGE AGREEMENT

NO CURE NO PAY

Date

On board the yacht

IT IS HEREBY AGREED BETWEEN

(afterwards called "the Master") and

(afterwards called "the Contractor") as follows:

1. The Contractor agrees to use his best endeavours to salve the
and take her into

or other place to be hereafter agreed with the Master providing at his own risk all proper assistance and labour. The services shall be rendered and accepted as salvage services upon the principle of "no cure no pay" and the Contractor's remuneration in the event of success shall be £
— or if no sum be herein named such sum as may be decided by subsequent arbitration in accordance with the terms of Clause 3 herein.

2. The Contractor may make reasonable use of the vessel's gear anchors chains and other appurtenances during and for the purpose of the operations but shall not unnecessarily damage abandon or sacrifice the same or any other of the property.

3. Any question or difference at any time arising out of this agreement whether as to construction or otherwise or the operations thereunder shall be referred to arbitration by a sole arbitrator to be nominated by agreement between the parties hereto or in default of agreement by an arbitrator to be appointed by the secretary of Lloyd's. Any award by arbitration shall be final and binding on the parties hereto and the arbitrator shall have power to obtain call for receive and act upon any such oral or documentary evidence or information (whether the same be strictly admissible as evidence or not) as he shall think fit. Save as aforesaid the statutory provisions as to arbitration for the time being in force in England shall apply.

4. All costs of and incidental to any arbitration shall be paid by such of the parties hereto as the arbitrator shall direct.

Signatures of Master and Contractor

....

....

original owner can lay claim to it *after* salvage money
has been paid.

You should notify the insurance company of a
wreck as soon as possible and arrange at the same
time for the Receiver of Wrecks, H.M. Customs,
Police and, where appropriate, the relevant harbour
authority, to be informed. In certain cases, a stranded
wreck that dries *must* be notified to harbour
authorities and the Hydrographic Department, and
there may be costs in connection with its removal. For
example, in the Thames a wreck that obstructs a
shipping channel may be removed at your expense. In
the *Snark* case it was held that an owner was under a
duty to buoy or mark a wreck, and that if the
authority had to move it they could subsequently sell
it and recover their expenses from the proceeds.
Usually, however, an insurance company in possession
of all the facts will act on your behalf to avoid these
pitfalls.

Wreck management

A damaged boat lying on its side high up on an
accessible beach is a magnet to the curious. People
will want to touch it, be photographed alongside it,
climb all over it and liberate anything that is not
nailed down. Some kind of deterrent will be required
to keep them at bay, and the only variety that really
works is to have human beings on display for twenty-
four hours a day. Once it is seen that the wreck is
unattended, the progression from souvenir hunter to
determined looter will take place with frightening
speed. Boarding an abandoned wreck seems to give
enormous strength and inculcate intense greed in

otherwise mild and law-abiding persons, as the following tale may confirm.

I once went out as a salvager to a motor vessel that had been in collision, was abandoned by the crew and had drifted ashore in thick fog. We were the second boat there, and I was utterly astounded to see two old-age pensioners, who had rowed out in a dinghy, making off with the standard compass, complete with binnacle, and the captain's safe weighing in total about 136 kilograms. To this day, I don't know how they managed it.

The lesson, therefore, is to organize a rota of crew members and relatives, and ask Police and Customs officers to show themselves at the site at regular intervals. Sometimes, it may be necessary to enlist the help of bystanders to carry salvaged equipment up above the high-water mark, and here a useful piece of applied psychology comes into play. If equipment is left scattered about someone will make off with it. If, however, it is marshalled into neat piles, and covered with a sail or awning and lashed down, no one will touch it. Certain bits of gear left lying about have a special attraction to the light-fingered. Outboard motors, VHF sets, oars, boathooks and coils of rope must be locked away in a shed or motor vehicle as soon as they come ashore.

Aftermath

Insurance companies like to have full reports, including diagrams, before they shell out, and if the boat was wrecked returning from abroad the Customs will require the second part of Form C.1328 even though all you have brought ashore is a few soggy cigarettes. With a total loss, have the yacht particulars deleted from the Yacht and Boat Safety Scheme. Inform the Royal Yachting Association if the craft had been recorded in the Small Ship Register, and the Registrar-General of Shipping at Cardiff if it was a British-registered ship. Finally, mull over the whole episode and see where you went wrong. Losing your boat is a humbling experience, but you may be a better seaman thereafter.

INDEX